GTA 21-03-014
APRIL 2013

CONTENTS

APRIL 2013

PRIMER: CROSS CULTURAL COMPETENCE

Figures

4

APRIL 2013

Tables

Figure 1. Map of Iran

APRIL 2013

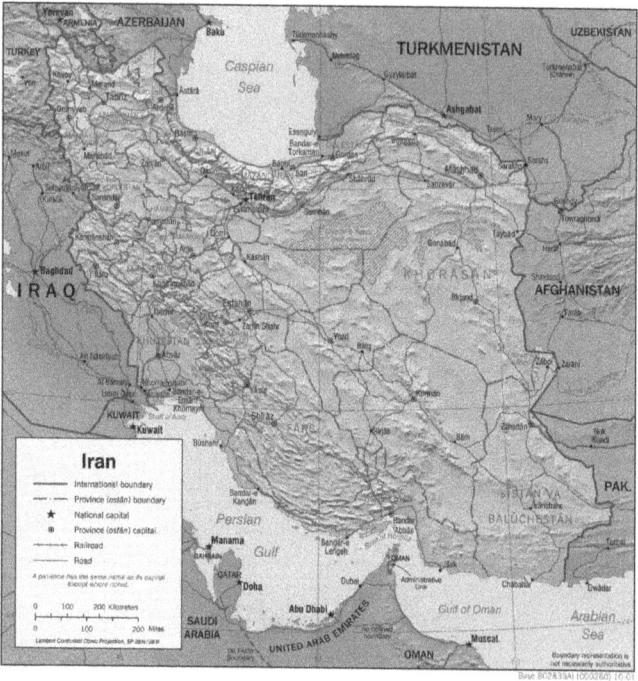

APRIL 2013

INTRODUCTION AND GEOGRAPHY

Geostrategic Overview

Iran is a regional power in the Middle East. It is the second largest producer of crude oil in the world and sits atop 10% of the world's proven oil reserves (the third largest). It is the second largest country in the Middle East in terms of population (79 million) and the third largest economy ($474 billion).[1] Geographically, Iran borders the Persian Gulf and the vital Straits of Hormuz —through which almost 20% of the world's oil production flows daily.

Today, Iran's area of influence extends west to Lebanon (with substantial influence in Iraq and Syria); south into the Persian Gulf; north into the Caspian Sea region; and east into western Afghanistan.

Politics in Iran is dominated by a conservative Muslim Shiite clergy. The current Iranian regime champions the cause of Shiite Muslims worldwide and competes with the Kingdom of Saudi Arabia for leadership in the Muslim world. The regime is seeking to extend its power in the region to assure the survival of its revolutionary Is-

---

[1] Egypt (83 million) has a larger population. Turkey ($762 billion) and Saudi Arabia ($588 billion) have larger GDPs (based on current exchange rates) although Iran's economy is slightly larger than Saudi Arabia based on CIA purchasing power parity estimates. (Statistics are taken from CIA Factbook. GDP statistics are 2012 estimates and population statistics are 2011 estimates.)

7

lamic theocracy.

U.S. policy makers are concerned about Iran's sponsor-ship of terrorism and aspirations to acquire nuclear weapons. A nuclear armed Iran could destabilize the vital Middle East oil-producing region and threaten Is-rael, a longtime U.S. ally. U.S. economic sanctions have been imposed on Iran since 1979. The current sanctions are the most wide-reaching to date.

Generally, sentiment of the Iranian population towards the U.S. is negative, stemming from the U.S. support of the former Pahlavi Shahs, who were unpopular in Iran. In the 1970s, the U.S. viewed the Pahlavi regime as a major ally who could assure security in the Persian Gulf region. U.S. diplomatic relations with Iran was cut in 1980, following the seizure of U.S. Embassy personnel as hostage in Tehran and has yet to be reestablished.

Geography [2]

Area: 1.6 million sq km (636,295 sq mi, about the size of Alaska).
Arable land: 9.78% of the country.
Terrain: North and west are mountainous; the large central plateau is desert. Two major mountain ranges are the Zagros, running parallel with the Iraqi border, and Alborz (Elburz) in northern Iran. Iran is in a high seismicity zone and subject to major earthquakes.
Climate: Semiarid; subtropical along the Caspian coast.

Major Cities:
Tehran is the political, administrative, industrial, and commercial center of Iran with a population of about 12 million in the greater metropolitan area (about one-sixth of the Iranian population). About one-fifth of Iran's manufacturing is located in the municipal area.
Esfahan is located in central Iran with the second largest urban population of about 3.4 million and historically was the Sassanid capital.
Mashhad (meaning "place of martyrdom") is located in Khorasan Province near the Turkmenistan border with a population of over 2.6 million. This city contains the

[2]Statistics and estimates from https://www.cia.gov/library/publications/the-world-factbook/geos/sa.html

9

famous shrine of Imam Reza and is a major pilgrimage site for Shiite Muslims.

Shiraz is located in Fars Province, the cultural cradle of Persian culture, and the economic center of southern Iran with a population of about 1.5 million.

Tabriz is located near the Azerbaijan and Armenian borders. It is the major Azeri city in Iran (where most of the population speaks both Azeri and Farsi) with a population of about 1.4 million.

Qom, located about 100 miles southwest of Tehran, is a holy city for Shiite Muslims – the birth place of Fatima and also the location of the premier Shiite institute of religious learning, the Howzeh-ye Elmieh – having a population of about 1 million.

10

History
Table 1. History

History
Timeline: Iran (Persia)

(1000 Before Current Era, BCE ca.)	Aryan tribes migrate into Iranian Plateau and Afghanistan Median Confederation
550-330	**Achaemenid Empire** (first Persian Empire)
330	Alexander the Great conquers Persian Empire
312-63	Seleucid-Hellenistic Empire
247 BCE- 224 (CE)	Parthian Empire
224-651	**Sassanid Empire**
663-750	Umayyad Caliphate (Islam introduced)
750-1258	Abbasid Caliphate
900s	Modern Farsi – adopt Arabic script
1220	Invasion by Genghis Khan (Mongol)
1370-1405	Timurid Empire

11

Table 1 History (continued)

1501-1736	**Safavid Dynasty** (Shiism becomes dominant)
1639	Treaty of Qasr-e Shirin (ends 150 years of war against Ottoman Empire)
1785-1925	**Qajar Dynasty** (start of modernization)
1828	Iran cedes control of Caucasus to Russia (Second Russo-Persian War)
1907	Limited constitutional monarchy established
1925-1979	**Pahlavi Dynasty**
1935	Iran adopted as official name (formerly, Persia)
1953	CIA led coup overthrows popular Prime Minister Mossadeq
1973	Rise in oil prices leads to unprecedented prosperity and Westernization
1978-79	Invasion by Genghis Khan (Mongol)
1979-present	**Islamic Republic**

Table 1 History (continued)

1979-1981	US Embassy personnel taken hostage (444 days)
1980-1988	Iran-Iraq War
1988	USS Vincennes mistakenly shoots down Iranian airliner
1989	Ayatollah Khomeini dies - Khamenei appointed supreme leader
1995	U.S. imposes oil/trade sanctions over Iranian sponsorship of terrorism
1999	Student pro-democracy demonstrations in Tehran
2002	Iran is named as part of the "axis of evil" by the Bush Administration
2002	Russian technicians construct nuclear reactor
2003	Student protest against Iranian clerical establishment
2006	UN Security Council impose sanctions on sensitive nuclear material
2009	Demonstrations over alleged vote-rigging
2010	U.S. imposes unprecedented sanctions

13

APRIL 2013

Ancient

Iran (historically known as Persia) is one of the world's
oldest continuous major civilizations, with over 4,000
years of written history. The Iranians are an Aryan people (Iran meaning "land of the Aryans") who first established themselves in present day Iran in about 1000 BCE
(Before Common Era). A united Median state was
formed after the dissolution of the Assyrian Empire in
about 616 BCE.

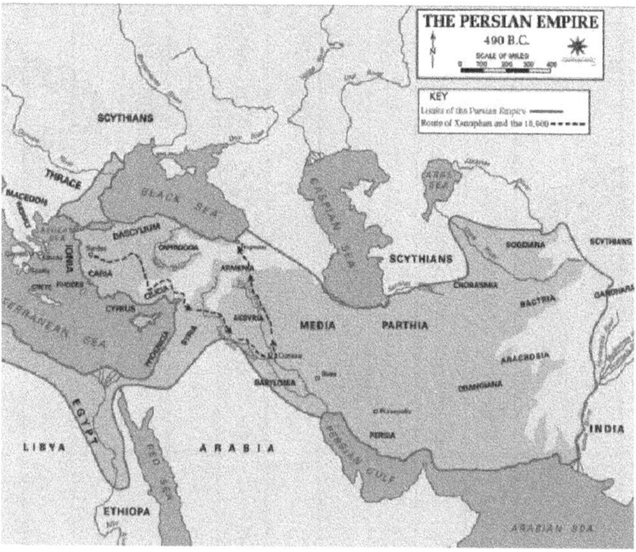

Figure 2 Map of Persian Empire 490 B.C.

14

The Achaemenid Persian Empire (arising from present day Pars Province in south central Iran) was founded by Cyrus the Great in the 6th Century BCE and is remembered for the high point of Persian greatness. The Empire was conquered by Alexander the Great in 330 BCE, followed by the Hellenistic Seleucid (312 to 63 BCE) and then the heterogeneous Parthian Empire, 247 BCE to 224CE ("Current Era").

The Sassanid Empire (224 to 651 CE) revived the flowering of Achaemenidian culture. The Arabs invaded Persia in 633 CE, bringing Islam to the area. Persian, as well as Hellenistic culture, contributed to the Islamic Golden Age under the Abbasid Caliphate. Persia was incorporated into the Seljuk Empire in the 11th and 12th centuries CE followed by an invasion by Mongol forces in the 13th century.

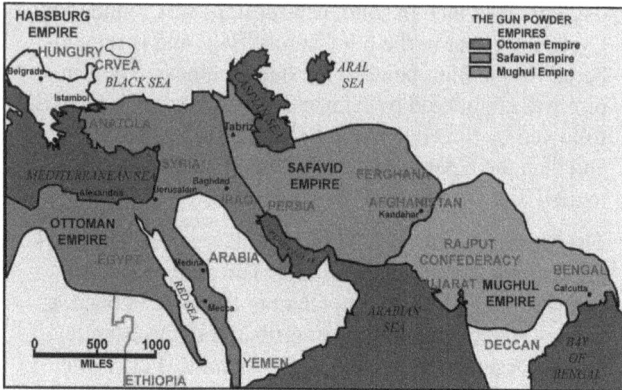

Figure 3 Map of the Gunpowder Empire

Persian unity was reestablished under the Safavid Dynasty (1501to1736), a "gunpowder empire," having won the territory back by means of newly-developed firearms. The Safavid were of Turkic and Azeri origins. Shia Islam became the dominant religion in Persia during their rule. Following the assassination of the last Safavid ruler, a politically chaotic period followed until the Qajar dynasty was established (1785 to1925).

APRIL 2013

Modern

Under the Qajars, Persians began adopting Western institutions and science. Persia entered a period of decline under pressure from the rising Russian and British Empires. A nationalist uprising against the Qajar Shah in 1905 resulted in the establishment of a limited constitutional monarchy in 1906. In 1907, Great Britain and Russia divided Persia into separate spheres of influence. The British discovered oil in Persia in 1908 and gained oil rights in exchange for payment of 16% of the annual profits to Persia.

Although neutral in World War I, Persia was occupied by Russian, British, and Ottoman forces. Following a period of instability after the war, Reza Khan, a military officer, seized control of the government in 1921. Reza Khan ousted the last ruler of the Qajar dynasty and declared himself Shah (1925to1941), establishing the Pahlavi Dynasty. In 1934, the international community formally recognized Persia by its native name, Iran. The Shah forcibly enacted policies of modernization and secularization in Iran and asserted government authority over the country's tribes and provinces. Many of his policies also created lasting resentment among devout Muslims and the clerical leadership.

17

During World War II, Great Britain and Soviet Union again occupied Iran. Reza (Khan) Shah was forced to abdicate in favor of his son, Mohammad Reza Pahlavi, who favored Great Britain over Germany.

In 1951, the Iranian parliament (*Majles*) voted to nationalize the oil industry and elected Mohammad Mossadeq as Prime Minister. Mossadeq, backed by popular support, clashed with the Shah over policy and power. Influenced by the British, the U.S. became concerned about communist influence in the Mossadeq government. The CIA engineered a coup that ousted Mossadeq in 1953. The Shah regained and expanded his powers and became a staunch U.S. ally against the Soviet Union.

Figure 4 U.S. President Nixon and Iranian Shah Pahlavi.

18

In 1961, the Shah carried out a series of economic, social, and administrative reforms, known as the "White Revolution." An unprecedented period of economic growth and modernization followed the tripling of oil revenues in 1973.

The Shah's repressive methods and rapid Westernization alienated large segments of the population. The conservative religious leader, Ayatollah Ruhollah Khomeini, led an Iranian Islamic Revolution that resulted in the exile of the Shah in 1979.

Figure 5 Supreme Leader Ayatollah Khomeini.

19

Ayatollah Khomeini became the Supreme Leader and advocated the ideology of *velayat-e faqih* (Guardianship of the Islamic Jurist, or scholar). The new constitution established the position of an Islamic jurist as the Supreme Leader and a Council of Guardians with powers to veto un-Islamic legislation and screen candidates for public office. The Council of Guardians could disqualify any candidates they deemed to be un-Islamic.

A consequence of the Iranian Islamic Revolution was the inspiration of Islamic movements throughout much of the Muslim world, leading to strife between Sunni and Shiites and heightening Iran's rivalry with the Kingdom of Saudi Arabia (the main champion of Sunni Islam).

On November 4, 1979, Iranian militant students seized the U.S. Embassy in Tehran and held 52 Americans hostage for 444 days. The takeover of the Embassy became a focal point for generating a new national unity and venting anger at the United States for its role in supporting the Shah. The U.S. launched a failed attempt (Operation Eagle Claw) to rescue the hostages. The hostages were released on January 21, 1981, minutes after Ronald Reagan was inaugurated as President of the United States.

20

From 1980 to 1988, Iran fought a bloody, indecisive war
with Iraq. To assure the flow of oil through the Persian
Gulf, the United States carried out naval escort, antimin-
ing, and special force operations (1987to1988) and conducted retaliatory strikes against Iranian oil platforms in
the Gulf. During these operations, the *USS Vincennes*
accidentally shot down an Iranian civilian airliner. A
cease fire was signed between Iran and Iraq on August
20, 1988.

After Ayatollah Khomeini's death on June 3, 1989, the
Assembly of Experts elected Ali Khamenei to be the
new Supreme Leader – a position he occupies today.
Politics has been dominated by conservatives who support the clergy. They have been challenged by moderate
elements that have been repressed from time to time. A
period of liberalization occurred under President
Mohammad Khatami (1997 to 2005) but has since been
reversed under the current President, Mahmoud Ahmadinejad (2005 to 2013).

IRANIAN CULTURAL BELIEFS

Iranian Identity

Identity as Iranian is rooted in being heirs to the Persian civilization and cultural traditions, which predates Islam. Pride in their imperial past is shared by about 85% of the Iranian population today. The Farsi (Persian) language is also central to Iranian identity. Identity with Persian culture is expressed in their love of traditional art and poetry, and in sophisticated traditional Persian manners.

Other elements of Iranian identity are their religion (Shia Islam) and nationalism linked to the Iranian state, particularly in terms of remembrance of historical domination by foreign powers. Despite invasions by Arabs, Seljuk Turks, Mongols, and more recently, hegemonic influence by Western Powers, Iranians have always reasserted their national identity.

At the personal level, the family and status are the most important. Identity progressively radiates out to the village, tribe/province, and the nation (the Iranian people).

22

Religion

Islam is the religion of over 98% of Iranians — 89% Shias, 9% Sunnis, and 2% belonging to other religions (Zoroastrian, Jewish, Christian, Baha'i). The official religion of Iran is Twelver Shia Islam (described below). Iran's Constitution also officially recognizes Christianity, Judaism, and Zoroastrianism, whose followers, according to the Constitution, are free to follow their own religion. Under the Constitution there are two seats reserved for Armenians (Christians), and one each for Assyrians (Christians), Jews, and Zoroastrians. A few Sunnis represent Sunni areas although there is no provision for Sunni representation in the Constitution.

Since the Islamic Revolution, the Iranian government has created a repressive atmosphere for nearly all non-Shia religious groups. Conversion from Islam to another religion is forbidden by the Constitution and may be punishable by death.

Islam—Basic Beliefs and Practices: *Islam* means "submission" to God, and *Muslim* means "one who submits." The religious tradition of Islam is based on the revelations received by Muhammad, considered by Muslims to be the final prophet of God. These cumulative revelations are known as the *Qur'an* ("recitation").

23

Islam understands itself as comprising a total way of life. All aspects of human activity are to be guided by *Shari`a*, which literally means the "path," consisting of God's intentions, expectations, and values by which humanity should live. As such, *Shari`a* is far wider than any legal code. However, Islamic jurisprudence (*fiqh*) seeks to approximate *Shari`a* in a practical, codified way, and many use the word *Shari`a* to refer to the laws of *fiqh* for a particular time and place.

The Qur'an and the Sunna (normative sayings and practices of Muhammad and, for Shia, of the Imams) are the two most important sources of *fiqh*. In addition, Islamic legal scholars may appeal to analogy, consensus, custom, and independent legal reasoning in formulating Islamic law. There are four main Sunni *madhabs* (legal schools of thought) and one major Shia one, whose differences result primarily from the varying relative weights each gives to the individual sources of *fiqh*. The laws of Muslim-majority countries generally seek explicitly to be in accordance with *Shari`a*, although governmental and legal structures may differ significantly among these countries.

The five practices (often called the Five Pillars) all Muslims consider obligatory are:

- *Shahadah*: The double profession that "There is no

24

god but God, and Muhammad is the messenger of God." To that common core, Shias permit (but do not require) the addition, "and Ali is his caretaker/ guardian."

- *Salat*: Formal prayer five times a day; Shias may combine the five prayers into three.
- *Sawm*: Fasting during daylight hours in the month of Ramadan, the 9th month of Islam's lunar calendar.
- *Zakat*: Obligatory donation to help the poor and needy.
- *Hajj*: Pilgrimage to Mecca at least once in a Muslim's lifetime, if financially and physically able, during a specified period in the 12th month of Islam's calendar.

The two major branches of Islam are: the Sunni (comprising about 85 %) and the Shia (about 15%), with the latter concentrated particularly in Iran, Iraq, Azerbaijan, Bahrain, Lebanon, and Yemen. The division between Sunnis and Shias originated over a dispute regarding who should succeed Muhammad after his death and, more importantly, over the nature of that leadership. Shias maintained that leadership of the Muslim community should remain within the household and lineage of Muhammad, and that Muhammad specifically had appointed his son-in-law and cousin, Ali, to be his successor. Although Ali was ultimately selected as the fourth

25

caliph (successor) of Muhammad, the Shias (partisans of Ali) view him as the first legitimate leader of the Muslim community after Muhammad's death.

After the original split, Sunni Islam and Shia Islam developed in different directions, both legally and theologically. There is considerable diversity within each of these branches, including distinctive subgroups. Modern conflicts between Sunnis and Shias are often more the result of clashes over the political power of the groups in a specific area, rather than primarily over religious beliefs and practices.

Twelver Shia Islam: For Shias, leadership is primarily a matter of spiritual guidance that impacts all areas of life, exercised by a series of divinely-appointed Imams in the bloodline of Muhammad, each of whom is specifically identified by the preceding Imam. (The Shia use of "Imam" in this exalted sense should not be confused with the usual Sunni use of "imam" to refer to a local leader of prayer in a mosque.) According to Shia Islam, God specially endows Imams with knowledge and wisdom by which they guide the community.

Most Shias are part of Twelver Shia Islam (also known as the Imami or as Ithna Ashari), the predominant group in Iran. Other Shia subgroups include the Ismaili (also called Seveners) and the Zaydi (Fivers). These sub-groups differ as to which branch of Muhammad's subsequent family tree they emphasize, and they each have their own distinctive theological and legal traditions. Twelver Shias are so named because they maintain that there have been Twelve Imams, with the Twelfth Imam having gone into "occultation" (that is, being hidden by God), initially in about 874 CE (with communication through a deputy), but with no further communication since about 941 CE, until he reappears as the Mahdi, just prior to the Day of Judgment, to bring about justice and peace on earth.

For Twelver Shias, Imams are necessary for providing ongoing guidance. However, since the current Imam is Hidden, religious scholars (*ulama*) have gradually assumed more and more authority, making Shia Islam more hierarchical than Sunni Islam. For most of Shia history, the authority of the *ulama* has not included political authority. However, in the period leading up to the Iranian Revolution in 1979, Grand Ayatollah Ruhollah Khomeini developed the doctrine of *vilayat-i faqih* (Guardianship of the Jurist), which maintains that, in the visible absence of the Imam, national governance best belongs in the hands of an Islamic legal scholar. A somewhat modified version of this provides the framework for the present Iranian Constitution, which was established after the Revolution.

27

A Shia religious scholar must be a *mujtahid*, that is, a person who has completed the necessary course of study at a *hawza* (Shia religious seminary), and has been certified as an Islamic jurist, qualified to exercise *ijtihad* (independent legal reasoning). Shias without those qualifications are expected to seek out the person they view as the most learned in religious law, and to follow that scholar as their *marja-i taqlid* (reference point for imitation). Scholars whom people view as their *marja* are called "Grand Ayatollahs," and usually teach at a *hawza*. People are free to make their own decision on their *marja*, based on a scholar's academic training, scholarly attainment, and positive reputation among both laypeople and other religious scholars. The resulting hierarchy of scholars is an informal, honorific one and not rigidly structured. Allegiance to various particular Grand Ayatollahs creates multiple networks of influence and competition among the Shia *ulama* and within the Shia community.

CUSTOMS AND ENGAGING IRANIANS

Customs

Good manners are deeply rooted in Iranian culture.
Foremost good manners include demonstrating respect
for elders, teachers, parents, and one's superiors.

Taboos for Muslims:

- Pork.
- Alcohol.
- Gambling.
- Intoxicants.
- Premarital sex, adultery, homosexuality, and abortion.
- Dogs are unclean.
- Idolatry—associating anything with Allah.
- Bodily fluids, such as blood, semen, etc., are unclean.
- Muslim woman marrying a non-Muslim.
- Charging interest.

A few Dos and Don'ts in Iran:

- *Do* remove your shoes when visiting a mosque or other Islamic religious building.
- *Do* signal a person by putting your hand out, palm side down, and curling your fingers.
- *Don't* walk in front of anyone praying.

29

APRIL 2013

- *Don't* point the sole of your shoe or foot at anyone.
- *Don't* sit next to a member of the opposite sex in public who is not your spouse or close relative.
- *Don't* ask an Iranian about his wife or any female relative.
- *Don't* hold hands in public or engage in other public displays of affection with the opposite sex.
- *Don't* give the "thumbs up" gesture.

Ta'arof ("mutual knowledge") is an Iranian formal etiquette or ritual courtesy based on deference to social rank and humility. One is expected to act with great hospitality, deference, and humility and *implied* is the understanding that one is doing so. For example: the senior may pause at a door for the junior in rank to pass. After a series of "you first/please yourself" (*befarma'id*), the senior will then enter or will sometimes insist that the junior enter to underline his authority.

Common words used in *ta'arof:*[3]
- *Ghabeli nadare* = It's not a big deal.
- *Ghadamet ro chesham* (you can walk on my eyes) = I am small in your presence. (you are very welcome to us)
- *Ghorbanet beram* (I will sacrifice myself for you) = Thank you very much.

[3]Passage adapted from Wikipedia, "Ta'arof". http://en.wikipedia.org/wiki/Taarof (Accessed 8 November 2012)

APRIL 2013

- *Cheshmet roshan* (light in your eyes) = You're worth it
- *Khaesh mikonam* (I do kindness) = You are humbling me

Indirect requests are often made indirectly to avoid a refusal or harm a relationship. These requests can be subtle and difficult for an American to pick up on. For example, if someone explains a problem they are having, they may be indirectly asking you to help with the problem.

Invitations or gifts may be offered with no expectation that they will be accepted. Invitations repeated only once generally have only a ritually polite meaning and are not "real" invitations. If someone really wants an offer to be accepted, they should repeat it two or three times. Something may be offered to a guest but should be refused (politely) at least once. If one admires something belonging to an Iranian, it is *ta'arof* for the host to offer the object to the admirer. However, unless it is a relative or very close friend, the guest should politely thank the host and refuse the gift.

Gift-Giving: [4] Iranians often give gifts on special occasions or for congratulations on an event such as graduation or a promotion. Always bring a small gift when you visit someone's house. The most typical gifts a visitor brings are flowers for the host or special sweets and pastries. It is customary to apologize when giving gifts for the gift being too small or too inexpensive. Gifts should be carefully wrapped and are usually not opened when received. Gifts are given more in social rather than in business situations. Gifts given in business situations or during negotiations could be construed as a bribe. It is not uncommon for businessmen to bring sweets and cakes to the office rather than bringing gifts.

Gender Relations: Iranian culture is patriarchal. The oldest male is dominant. The primary role of women is that of wife and mother. The father or husband makes most financial decisions, many times consulting with his male relatives about financial matters rather than with his wife. Women have a limited presence in public life, but they do vote and have greater discretion than women in many Islamic countries.

Males and females are sensitive about maintaining a physical boundary in public. Men and women typically

[4]Passage taken from Defense Language Institute, *Farsi Cultural Orientation* (October 2011), pp.37-38.

APRIL 2013

do not display affection in public, even if they are married. However, individuals of the same sex are much more physically interactive in public and routinely touch and may even hold hands or kiss on the cheeks.

Males are highly protective of female family members as this relates to family honor. It is therefore taboo to stare at or ask questions about female family members. Male and female honor and reputation must be protected and shame avoided in the public sphere.

Under the Shah, gender roles became more westernized and relaxed. However, the current Islamic government expects more traditional Islamic gender behavior. Current laws require women to observe *hijab* (dress code requiring women to cover their bodies except their face), although some women are daring in interpreting what they can wear. Recently, the "morality police" have enforced the laws on lax moral standards and forcibly closed coffee shops on grounds of violation of the dress code. During July 2012, the Government morality police raided 87 restaurants and coffee shops for violation of female dress codes.

Many restaurants have separate areas for males and females. In private homes, males and females are also often segregated during meals. On public transportation,

Iranian women may not sit next to men who are not relatives. Although women give their tickets to a bus driver
through the front door, they do not enter through that
door. Rather, women must go to their separate entrance
at the middle of the bus. [5]

Traditional Personal Relations:

Family: Iranians view the family as the utmost important aspect of life. Unmarried children live with their
parents even into older age, as living life outside of the
family is inconceivable. After marriage families are expected to come together at least once a week for a communal meal. Nepotism is seen as a positive, as family
loyalty is a priority.

Individuals' lives are dominated by family and family
relationships. Girls tend to be more disciplined than
boys with more restrictions for girls with respect to individual freedoms, dress codes, and associations with the
opposite sex.

Marriages are usually arranged but with agreement between, not only the parents, but both the bride and
groom. Marriage is often to a cousin. Traditionally, a

[5]Defense Language Institute, Farsi Cultural Orientation (October
2011), p.35

34

first choice for a man was his father's brother's daughter. Arranged marriages are still common. After marriage a woman belongs to her husband's household. An ill- fated marriage is a social stigma felt by men and women alike.

Public and Private: Iranians make a sharp distinction between public and private. The public sphere is an arena where men dominate. In public, Iranians tend to conform to the societal "norms." In private, amongst family and close friends, they are "themselves" and women often have great influence. Houses generally are surrounded by walls that separate the private and public worlds.

Mosque Etiquette:[6] International visitors are welcome in many Iranian mosques as long as they adhere to the same protocol as worshippers.

Shoes must be removed before entering. All female visitors must be covered, usually don a *chador.* Be alert to the male and female worship areas in order to enter the correct one. Take care not to walk in front of someone praying, which would invalidate their prayer. Always ask before taking photographs.

[6]Passage taken from Defense Language Institute, Farsi Cultural Orientation (October 2011), p.30-31.

APRIL 2013

Do not touch any books inside the mosque. Do not touch the walls, especially the western corner, where people direct their prayers. Some mosques have a shrine in the center or in one corner. Do not touch it. Do not speak unless you are spoken to and, even then, respond in a whisper. Large banners printed on a black or green background are displayed inside Shi'ite mosques. They may have messages of mourning or lamentations for a recently departed person. Do not touch or remove these banners.

Engaging Iranians

Attire:[7] There are highly specific codes of dress in Iran. Men traditionally should not wear shorts or even short sleeves, though today T shirts are not uncommon. Ties are seen as a symbol of westernization and are not worn by Iranians.

Women should take care to dress modestly. Women should wear a headscarf and be sure that arms and legs are completely covered. Bare legs or ankles should not be exposed. If wearing pants, remember to wear socks. Islamic dress is required for all women, including foreign tourists, although enforcement is selective.

[7]Passage taken from Defense Language Institute, Farsi Cultural Orientation (October 2011), p.36-37.

APRIL 2013

Greetings:[8] Shoes should be removed before entering a home. A pair of indoor slippers may be provided for guests. Iranians may stand close to you while talking. Do not back away as this can be misconstrued as rude.

When addressing someone for the first time use honorific pronouns and titles. Always greet elders first. Social protocol calls for one to stand when others enter any meeting space or area. The place furthest from the door is a place of honor. During a meeting it is not uncommon for people to wander in and out.

The custom of shaking hands in Iran varies throughout the country. When men are introduced, they generally shake hands. Another common form of greeting among men is the hug, usually three hugs while alternating shoulders. A kiss or two on each cheek is also common. These are normally reserved for persons that one has already met. Hand-kissing only occurs when a male religious follower visits his religious leader.

Among women, handshakes and hugs are common. The initial handshake should be light rather than firm. Women can also exchange a kiss on the cheek.

[8]Adapted from Defense Language Institute, Farsi Cultural Orientation (October 2011), p.33-34.

Do not shake hands or make any physical or eye contact in public with a member of the opposite sex. A slight bow as an acknowledgement at meeting is allowed. Any touching of a female by men who are not relatives is to be avoided. Women should not be alone in public with men unless they are relatives.

International visitors involved in social exchanges have reported being frequently approached by Iranian women. Caution is encouraged in such situations; although many laws are not strictly enforced, they are still on the books. The Iranian Revolutionary Guards, the law enforcement arm of the government, can detain anyone for any slight violation at any time.

Time: The concept of time in Iranian societies is much more relaxed than in Western societies. Meetings generally do not begin and end at a specific time, but Westerners should arrive at the specified time, as they are expected to be prompt. They may keep one waiting or cancel the meeting after arrival.
Government offices and many businesses close on Thursday afternoon and Friday. Saturday is the first day of the week. The work week usually is Sunday through Thursday and Friday is the Islamic day to visit the Mosque.

Building Rapport: Relationships and "face" are important in all interactions with Iranians. Drinking tea and
creating initial rapport are hugely important. Iranians
tend to avoid immediately delving into business. They
want to know the other's background and will provide
theirs as well. Flatter and expect to be flattered.

The tendency in Iran is to develop a relationship getting
to know and trust one another first, as is common to the
entire region. Decisions tend to be arrived at slowly and
generally only after trust has been established. Iranians
value patience and assume that the longer a negotiation
lasts the better the deal they will make.

It is rare for an Iranian to directly refuse or accept an
offer. It is important to understand this point and not get
upset or frustrated because a firm commitment is not
forthcoming. It is best to be patient and allow the process to continue. Getting upset, offending one's honor, or
breaking the relationship will generally end the process.

Iranians are more inclined to employ reason over emotion although many have a tendency to persuade using
emotion. They will generally choose long-term relationships over the best logical deal, differing from what is
often the practice in the West.

39

Conflict is to be avoided, and criticism is generally indirect. Iranians are methodical, well-prepared, and legalistic in their negotiation style. However, they are also indirect and full of contextual nonverbal clues. Iranians take pride in their ability to haggle. They like to build their arguments with anecdotes and analogies until they reach their main point which demonstrates their rhetorical abilities. Also, they find no problem with threats, disinformation, and bluffing in a negotiation. They are ultimately pragmatic in the sense of *realpolitik* and like to keep their options open.

Conversational Topics: Iranians are proud of their country, culture, and history. Men are often interested in soccer or other sports. They are encouraged to talk about their family, countries visited, and food. Many Iranians would like to send their children to American universities, so talk about American cities. Iranians tend to love poetry and most can recite the poetry of Rumi, Khayyam, Ferdowsi, Hafez, Saadi, or their modern favorites. Do not stray into conversation topics that could be deemed sensitive such as politics or religion. It is best to avoid questions about Islam, women, and their government until you have created a solid relationship.[9]

[9]Defense Language Institute, Farsi Cultural Orientation (October 2011), p.34.

40

A foreign woman in the company of a man may notice that most or all of the conversation is directed at the man. The woman may not even be acknowledged. Foreign females may find that they are given a kind of "honorary male" status and be allowed to mingle in places where Iranian women are forbidden, including tea houses. However, women should not count on this. Although many Iranian men are accustomed to dealing with foreign women, it should not be assumed that the men will follow Western conventions in their interactions.[10]

Meals: The main meal of the day is around 1 o'clock in the afternoon and is always preceded by ceremonious hand-washing and the serving of tea.

The traditional Iranian dinner is set out on a large white cloth spread over a carpet. The diners assemble around the cloth on soft cushions. An honored guest is seated at the head of the table.
It is customary to eat all foods with the fingers of the right hand. Special short-handled spoons are used for soups and soft desserts, and sometimes visitors are given forks. The food is prepared and served in such a way that knives are never needed or used at the table. Meat

[10]Defense Language Institute, Farsi Cultural Orientation (October 2011), p.36.

41

is usually used more as a condiment than as a focus of the meal and is eaten with a fork. Rice is often eaten with a spoon.

As a guest, you will be asked to start eating before the others. When asked if you want more of anything, you should always decline even if you want more. This gives the host or hostess a chance to insist that you have more. After having declined at least twice, you are then expected to accept. Since this pattern is reciprocal, anything you wish to give someone should be offered several times.

After you have finished, emphasize how much you enjoyed everything that was served. In return, the hosts

Figure 6 Iranian family eating a meal.

42

will keep apologizing for serving mediocre fare and in such limited variety. This is common modesty and should not be taken seriously.

The Iranian national dish, called *chelow kabab,* consists of a filet of lamb marinated in lemon juice or yogurt, onions, and saffron. A common drink with a meal is dough, a preparation of yogurt and salted water that is similar to Turkish *ayran,* Lebanese *lebni,* and Indian *lassi.*

43

Strategic Culture[11]

Way of War: The Iranian "way of war" has been shaped by its cultural identity as a great power (desire for status and influence), being overrun by less developed civilizations (deterrence and defense), and historical isolation as a great power (self-reliance). As analyzed by Michael Eisenstadt, Iranian approaches to war are (extracts):

Proxy Warfare. The use of street mobs and violent pressure groups as instruments of domestic politics is an old tradition in Iran, going back at least to the Qajar dynasty. This form of "politics by other means" finds its corollary in Iran's use of militia and terrorist surrogates as an instrument of foreign policy.

Psychological, Moral, and Spiritual. The Islamic Republic of Iran (IRI) places great importance on the primacy of the moral and spiritual dimensions of war over the physical and technological. Whereas the United States undertakes information operations to support its military activities, Iran frequently undertakes military activities (such as exercises, shows of force, and proxy

[11]This section is extracted from Michael Eisenstadt's *The Strategic Culture of the Islamic Republic of Iran: Operational and Policy Implications.* Marine Corps University, 2011.

44

operations) to support its information operations. While military victories are certainly desired, the ultimate measure of the utility of force is whether it advances the IRI's interests, promotes its culture of resistance, jihad, and martyrdom, and yields an "image of victory."

The IRI has tried to "Islamize" the security forces and military along with nurturing a culture of resistance, jihad, and martyrdom. To this end, it has attempted to inculcate what it calls *Alavi* and *Ashurai* values in its fighting men—by extolling the heroic martial virtues of the Imam Ali and the complementary virtue of martyrdom. The doctrine of resistance *(moqavemat)* as practiced by the IRI assigns primary importance to the accomplishment of psychological effects. It assumes that victory is achieved by demoralizing the enemy—through terrorizing its civilians, bleeding its armies, and denying it battlefield victories. The IRI's efforts to promote a culture of resistance, jihad, and martyrdom are energized and strengthened by conflict. The Iranian Revolutionary Guard Corps (IRGC) has elevated the moral and spiritual dimension above all others in the belief that faith, ideological commitment, and religious zeal are the keys to victory.

Strategic Patience. The IRI prefers to avoid decisive engagements and head-on confrontations, and has repeatedly demonstrated a preference for strategies of delay, indirection, and attrition. This preference for strategies of indirection and attrition is well-suited to a culture that has a rather expansive concept of time, that values strategic patience, and whose senior political and military leaderships are characterized by a great deal of continuity. It is an alien way of thinking, however, for impatient Americans whose contemporary strategic culture emphasizes "surges," "decisive operations," and "exit strategies," whose political culture is shaped by the 24-hour news cycle. Iranians can look to Shiite history as well as their own cultural heritage for examples of the benefits of strategic patience.

Propensity to Overreach. The IRI has repeatedly demonstrated a tendency to overplay its hand in its diplomacy, business dealings, and military activities, such as to drag out negotiations "to the 61st minute" in the pursuit of minor advantage. One of the reasons that Iranian officials often find it difficult to close a deal or end a dispute is their zero sum approach to conflicts. This approach precludes compromise and the fear that in a political system characterized by extreme factionalism rivals will claim that they could have done better.

Calibrated Violence. When the IRI resorts to force, it generally does so in a calculated manner and often to achieve specific psychological effects—although at times it has acted in a less constrained manner.

46

Instruments of Soft Power: Cultural elements of
Iran's soft power are (extracts from Eisenstadt):

Diplomatic - Reputation and image management: Tehran presents itself as a dependable partner and danger-
ous adversary while pushing a triumphalist narrative
asserting that it is a rising power with God and history
on its side.

Informational: Iran vies for Arab "hearts and minds"
through Arabic-language news broadcasts reflecting
Tehran's propaganda line. The future prospects of
Iran's soft power will depend on the future direction of
Iraq-Iran relations, the overall tenor of Iran-Arab and
Sunni-Shiite relations in the Gulf in the wake of the
Saudi-led intervention in Bahrain, and the future status
of Iran's nuclear program, which may be Tehran's ulti-
mate psychological warfare enabler in the region and
beyond.

Military - Export of revolutionary Islam: Tehran seeks
the primacy of its brand of Islam in Shiite communities
around the world by spending prodigious sums of
money to support the activities of clerics trained in Qom
and steeped in the ideology of clerical rule, and by co-
opting or displacing clerics trained elsewhere (such as
Najaf). Tehran also seeks to create bonds of solidarity
with Shiite communities around the world that can serve

47

as external bases of support for its policies and as allies should it be attacked. Where there are embattled Shiite communities and weak states, Iran has created proxy militias, such as the Lebanese Hezbollah and various Hezbollah clones in Iraq—including Kataib Hezbollah Asaib Ahl al-Haqq, and the Promised Day Brigades—to defend the interests of the local Shiite community, to do its bidding, and to spread its culture of resistance, jihad, and martyrdom.

Economic leverage: Tehran pursues trade and investment with other countries for profit, fostering dependencies which it can exploit. In Iraq, for instance, it has used business deals to bolster local allies; dumped cheap, subsidized produce and consumer goods on the local market; and undercut Iraq's agricultural and manufacturing sectors.

48

STRUCTURES AND INSTITUTIONS

Political

Iran has been ruled since 1979 by a conservative clergy who are mostly opposed to Western secular values. Domestic Iranian politics is divided broadly between conservative Islamists and a more moderate "reform" faction. Former President Mohammad Khatami's support for greater social and political freedoms made him popular with the young--an important factor given around half of the Iranian population is under 30. His relatively liberal ideas put him at odds with the Supreme Leader, Ayatollah Khamenei, and hardliners committed to the Islamic ideology of *velayat-e faqih* and establishing an ideal Islamic community. Conservatives regained control of the government with the election of Mahmoud Ahmadinejad in 2005, and again in 2009. However, some of Ahmadinejad's more extreme policies reportedly have been limited by Khamanei.[12]

---

[12] Adapted from BBC, Iran Profile http://www.bbc.co.uk/news/world-middle-east-14541327 (accessed November 2012)

Table 2 Chief of State and Cabinet Members
of Foreign Governments

Chief of State and Cabinet Members of Foreign Governments
Date of Information: 6/11/2012

Supreme Leader	**Ali Hoseini-KHAMENEI,** *Ayatollah*
President (Pres.)	**Mahmud AHMADI-NEJAD**
Speaker of the Islamic Consultative Assembly (Majles)	**Ali Ardeshir-LARIJANI**
Secretary of the Cabinet	**Ali SADUQI**
Chief of Staff, Presidential Office, & Advisor to the Pres.	**Esfandiar Rahim MASHAIE**
First Vice President	**Mohammad Reza Rahimi**
Vice President for Atomic Energy	**Fereidun ABBASI-Davani**
Vice President for Cultural Heritage & Tourism	**Hasan MASAVI**
Vice President for Environmental Protection	**Mohammad Javad MOHAMMADIZADEH**
Vice President for Executive Affairs	**Hamid BAQAI**
Vice President for Implementation of the Constitution	**Mohammad Reza MIR-TAJODINI**

50

Table 2. Chief of State and Cabinet Members
of Foreign Governments
(continued)

Chief of State and Cabinate Members of Foreign Governments
Date of Information: 6/11/2012 (Continued)

Vice President for International Affairs	Ali SAIDLU
Vice President for Legal and Parliamentary Affairs	Lotfollah FARUZANDEH-Dehkardi
Vice President for Management Development and Human Resources	Ebrahim AZZI
Vice President for Maryrs and War Veterans Affairs	Masud ZARIBAFAN
Vice President for Planning and Strategic Supervision	Behruz Moradi
Vice President for Scientific and Technologic Affairs	Nasrin SOLTANKHAH
Minister of Agriculture Jihad	Sadeq KHALILIAN
Minister of Communications and Information Technology	Reza TAQI-PUR
Minister of Defense and Armed Forces Logistics	Ahmad VAHIDI
Minister of Econimic Affairs and Finance	Ali Akbar SALEHI
Minister of Health Treatment and Medical Education	Marzeih VAHID-DASTJERDI

51

Table 2 Chief of State and Cabinet Members
of Foreign Governments
(continued)

Chief of State and Cabinate Members of Foreign Governments
Date of Information: 6/11/2012 (Continued)

Minister of Industry, Mining and Trade	Mehdi QAZANFARI
Minister of Intelligence and Security	Heidar MOSLEHI
Minister of Interior	Mostafa Mohammad NAJAR, *Brig. Gen.(Ret)*
Minister of Islamic Culture and Guidance	Mohammad HOSEINI
Minister of justice	Morteza BAKHTIARI
Minister of Labor, Cooperatives, and Social Welfare	Abdol Reza SHEIKH-OL-ESLAMI
Minister of Petroleum	Rostam QASEMI, *Brig. Gen.*
Minister of Roads and Urban Development	Ali NIKZAD
Minister of Science, Research and Technology	Kamran DANESHJU
Minister of Sports and Youth	Mohammad ABBASI
Government Spokesman	

52

Table 2 Chief of State and Cabinet Members
of Foreign Governments
(continued)

Chief of State and Cabinate Members of Foreign Governments
Date of Information: 6/11/2012 (Continued)

Governor, Central Bank of Iran	**Mahmud BAHMANI**
Head of Interest Section in the US	**Mostafa RAHMANI**
Permanent Representative to the United Nations	**Mohammad KHAZAI-Torshizi**

https://www.cia.gov/library/publications/world-leaders-1/world-leaders-i/iran-nde.html

53

APRIL 2013

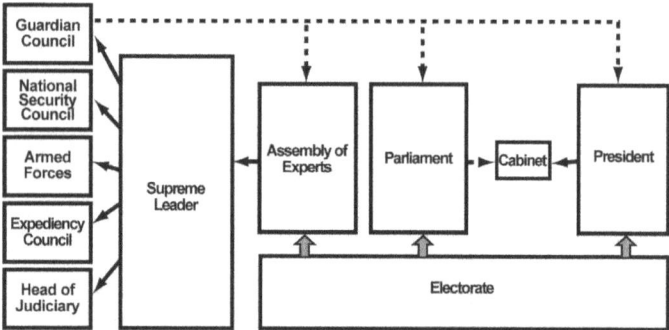

Figure 7 Governmental organization chart.
http://www.publications.parliament.uk/pa/cm200708/
cmselect/cmfaff/142/14207.htm

Central Government: The government structure in Iran is a unitary theocratic Islamic parliamentary republic – a theocracy (religious rule) with a supreme spiritual/political leader and clerics dominating the government. The current Iranian Constitution was ratified in December 1979 and revised in 1989.

Theocratic Guidance:

Supreme Leader supervises general government policy, commands the armed forces, can declare war,

54

APRIL 2013

accepts impeachment of the President, and has appointment powers including members of the Council of Guardians (half the members), Expediency Council judiciary, commanders of the armed forces and police, head of the Islamic Republic of Iran Broadcasting (IRIB), and heads of major religious foundations.

Assembly (Council) of Experts consists of 86 Islamic scholars (mujahids) who are directly elected; has the primary responsibility for selecting the Supreme Leader and to monitor his performance. The Assembly meets infrequently but is required to meet at least twice a year.

Council of Guardians has chief theocratic oversight functions: legislative, judicial, and electoral. The Council consists of 12 members: 6 Islamic scholars selected by the Supreme Leader and 6 elected by the legislature, *(Majlis)* upon nomination by the High Council of Justice (who is appointed by the Supreme Leader). It reviews statutes passed by the *Majlis* and can veto its statutes or approve them to become laws, along with interpreting the constitution. The Council qualifies candidate competency for election to the presidency, *Majlis,* and the Assembly of Experts.

55

Expediency Council may sustain or reject a Council of Guardian veto of statutes from the *Majlis*. Real power is thought to be as advisory council to the Supreme Leader. The Supreme Leader appoints the Council for a 5-year term. The number in the Council varies. Currently there are 33 members to serve from 2012 through 2017.

Executive/Government:

President is the head of government (and also appoints and receives ambassadors) but is subordinate to the Supreme Leader in foreign policy, over the armed forces, and nuclear policy. The President appoints ministers, chairs the Council of Ministers, negotiates treaties, and administers the national budget. The President is directly elected for a 4-year term for no more than two terms.

Council of Ministers consists of ministers who head the major government ministries. The President selects most ministers with legislative approval. The Supreme Leader effectively appoints some of the ministers to the more critical ministries.

Legislative: The *Majlis* (Islamic Consultative Assembly) is a unicameral legislative body with the power to initiate and pass laws, summon and impeach Cabinet Ministers and the President, approve the budget, and ratify

56

international treaties. The 290 *Majlis* members are elected for a 4-year term.

Judicial: The judiciary is independent of the executive and legislative branches. The judiciary is headed by the High Council of the Judiciary, whose superior is also head of the Supreme Court appointed by the Supreme Leader. The High Council also includes the Public Prosecutor General as well as three other members, serving for a 5-year term.

There are four general types of courts:
- *Public Courts:* civil and criminal cases.
- *Revolutionary Courts:* jurisdiction related to national security including narcotics smuggling and terrorism.
- *Special Clerical Courts:* criminal complaints against clerics.
- *Court of Administrative Justice:* complaints against the government.

The final appeals court is the Supreme Court (a constitutional court that applies the laws rather than interprets the Constitution; a power of the Council of Guardians). There is no appeal in the Revolutionary and Clerical courts. Since 1980, the judicial system has been "desecularized." Judges are either *mujtahid* or have demonstrated expertise in Islamic law.

57

Local Government: Iran is a unitary state. This means, unlike the federal system we have in the United States, policy and administrative control rests with the central government in Tehran. Provinces along with districts and villages are primarily administrative subdivisions of the central government.

Administrative Units: As of 2004, there are 31 provinces in Iran headed by a Governor General *(Ostandar)* nominated by the Ministry of Interior and appointed by the President. The five largest provinces by population are Tehran (25%), Khuzestan (15%), Esfahan (6%), and Korasan-e Razavi (5%). Provinces are further subdivided into counties and districts headed by governors appointed by the Ministry of interior.

Islamic Councils: The lowest units of local government are the town and village Islamic councils. According to the Constitution, Islamic Councils are the link between

Figure 8 Provinces of Iran.

the people and the state, although this process is still being resolved. As of 1999, the councils are locally elected. The council selects the Chairman and Mayor (Mayors are scheduled to be elected by popular vote starting with the 14 June 2013 elections).

59

APRIL 2013

Village Councils select the District Council from among their members. The District Council in turn selects the Provincial Council. Village and town councils focus on regional development and enforce the policies of the government at the local level.

Civil Society: Iranian civil society traditionally is patrimonial and currently dominated by the clergy linked to the state. Traditional and secondary association sectors outside of clergy dominated associations have little or limited influence government policy. The traditionally absentee landowner class was eliminated as a political force by the Shah's land reforms in the 1960s.

Patrimonialism: This refers to traditional authority organized as an extension of the household heading by a male. It tends to frame the leader as a father-like figure and subordinate authority relation of elder and junior male household heads throughout the society. The role of leadership is personal and hierarchical, and extends across political, military, social, and economic activities.

Clergy: Under the doctrine of *velayat-e faqih,* the clergy have the role of guardianship over Iranian society. While the clergy are not a monolithic block, their power, independent of the government, is based on religious foundations *(Bonyad),* their formal and informal roles as jurists, control over traditional religious institutions

60

(such as the Friday prayer), religious organizations, and their influence over the media.

Some have charged that the *Bonyads* (that control up to 20% of the economy) assist only groups that support the cleric dominated regime. The large national *Bonyads* inherited the assets from the Shah's foundations. Many local mosques have associated *Bonyads* that are recipients of the traditional Islamic *Khums* (in Shia tradition this is one-fifth of a business's profits).

Tribes: Tribalism in Iran diminished under the impact of urbanization, de-tribalization (private ownership) of pasture lands, and the Pahlavi Shahs' policies. According to the *Tehran Times* (6 Aug 2011), there are over 1.5 million nomadic tribesmen (where tribal tradition remains strong) spread across about a hundred tribes. At least that number of tribesmen recently settled in urban areas.

The most important tribes are the: Afshars and Shahsevans (Turkish in Azerbaijan Province), Bakhtiatis (likely Arabic descent in Khuzestan Province), Kurdish tribes, Baluch tribes (southeastern Iran), Lur tribes, Arabic tribes, and Turkmans (Khorassan Province).

NGOs: There are 2,500 to 8,000 nongovernmental organizations (NGOs) operating in Iran. NGOs had grown

APRIL 2013

under the more liberal policies of President Khatami but have since been discouraged by the current regime. NGOs in Iran are required to be "nonpolitical" and register with the Ministry of Interior. The types of NGOs include guild/business, labor unions, professional associations, youth, religious, sports, women, charities and foundations (mainly health related), and environmental.

Traditional Associations: There is a long tradition of cooperative associations in Iran. These include cooperatives for managing water resources, agricultural cooperatives (mainly labor exchange), savings cooperatives *(Qarz al hasaneh),* religious cooperatives (such as for *Ashura*), and funeral associations. These associations are semi-informal cooperatives formed in neighborhoods, villages, and among kin, and they are important sources of community cohesion and mobilization. Traditional associations tend to be present outside the state and modern sectors, and among the poor and rural communities.

Political Parties (CIA Factbook, 2012): Formal political parties are a relatively new phenomenon in Iran and most conservatives still prefer to work through political pressure groups rather than parties. Often political parties or coalitions are formed prior to elections and disbanded soon thereafter. A loose pro-reform coalition called the 2nd Khordad Front achieved considerable success in elections for the sixth *Majles* in early 2000. The coalition planned to participate in the seventh *Majles* elections in early 2004 but boycotted them after 80 incumbent reformists were disqualified.

A new conservative group, Islamic Iran Developers Coalition *(Abadgaran),* took a leading position in the new *Majles* after winning a majority of the seats in February 2004. After the 2008 *Majles* elections, traditional and hard-line conservatives attempted to close ranks under the United Front of Principlists and the Broad Popular Coalition of Principlists.

Several reform groups, such as the *Mojahedin* of the Islamic Revolution Organization (MIRO) and Islamic Iran Participation Front (IIPR), also came together as a reformist coalition in advance of the 2008 *Majles* elections. The IIPR has repeatedly complained that the overwhelming majority of its candidates were unfairly disqualified from the 2008 elections.

Political Pressure Groups (CIA Factbook, 2012):
Conservative supporters of the government
- Ansar-e Hizballah
- Follower of the Line of the Imam and the Leader
- Islamic Coalition Party *(Motalefeh)*
- Islamic Engineers Society
- Tehran Militant Clergy Association *(Ruhaniyat)*

Active pro-reform student group: Office of Strengthening Unity (OSU)

Opposition groups:
- Freedom Movement of Iran
- Green Path movement
- *Marz-e Por Gohar*
- National Front
- Various ethnic and monarchist organizations

Armed political groups:
- Democratic Party of Iranian Kurdistan (KDPI)
- *Jundallah* (Baloch-Sunni)
- *Komala (Kurdish)*
- *Mojahedin-e Khlaq* Organization (MEK or MKO) (leftist, was stationed at Camp Liberty)
- People's Free Life party of Kurdistan (PJAK)

APRIL 2013

International Relations:

Iranian Strategy: The strategic objectives of Iran's leadership has consistently been the survival of the regime; making Iran a dominant regional power; and turning the country into an economic, scientific, and technological powerhouse. Its principles of military strategy include deterrence, asymmetrical retaliation, and attrition warfare. Iran can conduct limited power projection with its strategic ballistic missile program and naval forces. Iran actively uses proxies, often terrorist groups, to further its foreign policy aims.

State Sponsor of Terrorism: The United States claims Iran supports Lebanese Hezbollah and Palestinian terrorist groups – notably, Hamas, the Palestinian Islamic Jihad, and the Popular Front for the Liberation of Palestine-General Command (PFLP-GC) – with funding, weapons, and training, along with providing sanctuary to terrorist groups from Iraq, Afghanistan, and Lebanon. In 2007 the United States added the Iranian government Islamic Republican Guard Corps (IRGC) to its list of foreign terrorist organizations.

Nuclear Policy: The dominant international and domestic political issue concerning Iran is its program of uranium enrichment and reprocessing activities, which the U.N. Security Council has called upon Iran to suspend.

Iran's refusal to comply resulted in international sanctions being imposed by a number of nations, which may have had a major impact on the human welfare and economy of Iran.

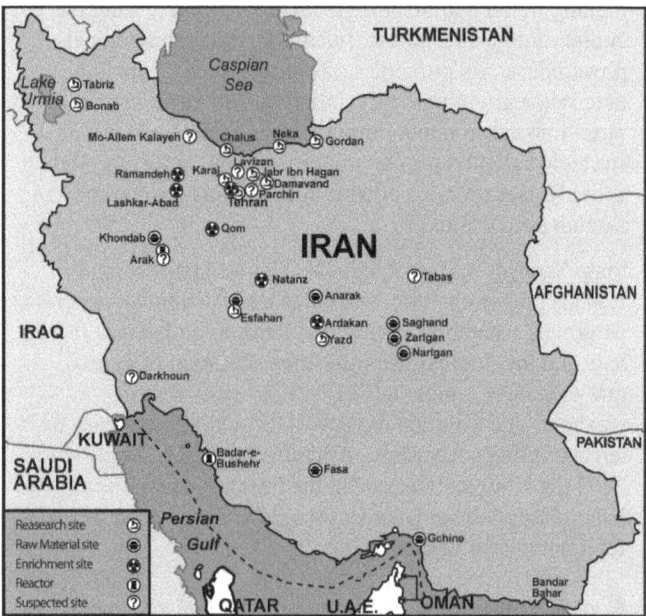

Figure 9 Iranian nuclear sites.

66

Military

The Supreme Leader is commander-in-chief of the armed forces, consisting of the regular military and the Islamic Revolutionary Guard Corps (IRGC). The military is primarily structured as a defense and deterrent force with an emphasis on asymmetric warfare. The military has very limited power projection capability. The Iranians are not known to have operational CBN programs although they are suspected of developing this capability. Iran has developed a cyber attack capability.

Regular Military Forces *(Artesh)*
The Islamic Republic of Iran Ground Force (IRIGF):
This comprises armored and infantry divisions, artillery groups, and an airborne division and commando division. IRIGF strength is 350,000 soldiers (an additional 100,000 to 125,000 in IRGC ground force). About 220,000 of the IRIGF are conscripts. Forces are not structured for deep project power but do have significant irregular warfare capability.
Tanks have limited capabilities and are mostly locally produced Zulfigars and some old (480) Soviet T-72. Most of the artillery weapons are from the Iran-Iraq War era. IRIGF has 1,000 to 1,560 armored personnel carriers and fighting vehicles, perhaps 40 attack helicopters, and about 300 transportation and utility helicopters.

LAND ARMY

Total Land Weapons: 12,393

Tanks: 1,793 [2011]

APCs / IFVs: 1,560 [2011]

Towed Artillery: 1,575 [2011]

SPGs: 865 [2011]

MLRSs: 200 [2011]

Mortars: 5,000 [2011]

AT Weapons: 1,400 [2011]

AA Weapons: 1,701 [2011]

Logistical Vehicles: 12,000

Figure 10 Iranian land army strength.

NAVAL POWER

Total Navy Shipss: 261

Merchant Marine Strength: [2011]

Major Ports and Terminals: 3

Aircraft Carriers: 0 [2011]

Destroyers:3 [2011]

Submarines: 19 [2011]

Patrol Craft: 198 [2011]

Mine Warfare Craft: 7 [2011]

Amphibious Assault Craft: 26 [2011]

Figure 11 Iranian naval strength.

Islamic Republic of Iran Navy (IRIN): IRIN (strength about 18,000 sailors and marines) has three Russian Kilo-class submarines and 4 to 7 midget submarines (and is reportedly building 4 more). The combat surface force consists of 4 frigates and 3 corvettes inherited from the Shah. In 2012 it deployed two separate groups to the Mediterranean.

The IRGC Navy (strength about 20,000) is responsible for Gulf operations. It has a large number of missile patrol crafts that can be employed in swarm attacks on surface vessels. They also have a significant mine warfare capability (estimated to have 2,000 mines by 2005). The IRGC Navy has land based anti-ship missile batteries with a 200 to 280 kilometer range as well as small mobile launchers. They also have amphibious lift capability for about a battalion.

The Islamic Republic of Iran Air Force (IRIAF): The Islamic Republic of Iran Air Force (IRIAF) is estimated to have 312 combat aircraft. Over 100 are U.S. aircrafts inherited from the Shah and about 80 aircraft are early export Russian models. According to Cordesman, "40 percent to 60 percent have no mission capability at any given time, and many are so old or poorly supported that they cannot sustain a high sortie rate."

Iran's air defense system has modern short-range manportable systems. Other air defense systems are obsolete and have limited capabilities against modern strike fighters, and cruise and air-to-surface missile attacks.

70

AIR POWER

Total Aircraft: 1,030 [2011]

Helicopters: 357 [2011]

Serviceable Airports: 319 [2011]

Figure 12 Iranian air strength.

Iran's Revolutionary Guard Corps (IRGC) *(Pasdaran)*

The IRGC (strength about 150,000) was formed by the former Supreme Leader Ayatollah Khomeini in 1979 as a militia to enforce Islamic control and has since been transformed into a regular active military force. The IRGC has land, naval, air, and intelligence branches, and control over the missile forces and the *Basij* militia. *Ansar Ul Mehdi* Corps within the IRGC is responsible for protection of top government officials. The IRGC controls companies with billions of dollars in assets (perhaps the third largest economic enterprise in Iran). It operates directly under the Supreme Leader and independently of the *Artesh.*

71

The IRGC also is responsible for irregular warfare for defending Iran as well as is Iran's most powerful internal security force. It has been responsible for suppressing ethnic and civil dissent. Some analysts consider the IRGC to be the second most powerful entity in Iran after the Supreme Leader. IRGC veterans won 182 of 290 seats in the *Majlis* in the 2008 election and currently occupy 9 of 21 ministry portfolios.

Basij: The *Basij* was established as a people's militia in 1980 and became an auxiliary militia force under the IRGC in 1981. The *Basij* militia played a noteworthy role in the Iran-Iraq war by launching human wave attacks and acting as human minesweepers. Also, they have been employed to put down protests, act as morality police, and engage in developmental activities.

The *Basij* (according to CSIS) is thought to have 90,000 active members, 300,000 reservists, and 1 million standby members. They claim to have 5 to11 million members. The Basij is organized nationally by resistance areas, from city down to cell. They are organized in 2,500 Al Zahra (all women) and Ashura battalions (male) (Radio Free Europe). While the rank and file member is thought to be paid little, they receive perks such as preferential entry to universities and for housing. *Basij* members are associated with *Ansar-e Hezbollah*, a

72

domestic vigilante group said to be financed and controlled by senior clerics.

Quds Force: This is an elite unit within the IRGC (strength variously estimated to be 5,000 to 15,000). While little is known about them, it is believed to be a clandestine special operations force supporting Islamic revolutions outside of Iran. *Quds* has offices in many Iranian Embassies. It supports the Hezbollah in Lebanon, Shiite militias in Iraq (including SCIR and JAM), and has supported the Northern Alliance in Afghanistan. *Quds* forces are believed to have plotted activities in the United States, India, and Venezuela as well as supported violent jihadist groups.

Missile Strategic Force: Iran has the largest missile force in the Middle East. It has several thousand short- and medium-range missiles, with a maximum range of 2,200 kilometers. The accuracy of the missiles is poor. Further development of its missile capability is believed to be central to Iran's deterrence strategy.

Other Security Forces:

Disciplinary Forces of the Islamic Republic of Iran: This is the national level police force and operates under the Ministry of Interior. It has about 45,000 to 60,000 men serving as police and border guards.

Ministry of Intelligence and Security (MOIS or VEVAK): Little is known from open sources about MOIS. Its charter is to gather and analyze domestic and international intelligence. U.S. Department of State (16 Feb 2012) claims MOIS supported "terrorist groups including al-Qaida, Hizballah, and Hamas" as well as the Syrian Assad Regime. The Department of Disinformation is said to be one of its largest departments. MOIS is believed by some analysts to be Iran's most powerful ministry.

74

Economy[13]

Overview: Iran's economy is characterized by a large hydrocarbon sector. The Iranian state plays a key role in the economy, owning large public and quasi-public enterprises (including the *Bonyads* and IRGC), which dominate the large-scale manufacturing and commercial sectors. The financial sector is also dominated by state-owned banks. The private sector is mostly limited to small-scale manufacturing, commerce, and agriculture. Iran has a substantial subsidy program for basic necessities like food and gas, which is funded mostly from oil revenues.

GDP: $482.4 billion (2011 est) at Purchasing Power Parity (PPP) $1.003 trillion (2011 est)
GDP per capita: $13,200 PPP (2011 est)
GDP real growth rate: 2%. (2011 est)
GDP composition by sector: Agriculture 10.4%, industry 37.7%, services 51.8% (2011 est)
Labor force: 26.4 million (2011 est); by occupation: Agriculture 25%, industry 31%, services 45% (June 2007)
Unemployment rate overall: 15.3% (2011 est); 15-24 years: 23%
Population below poverty line: 18.7% (2007 est)
Inflation Rate: 22.5% (2011 est)

[13]All numbers and estimates from https://www.cia.gov/library/publications/the-world-factbook/geos/sa.html

Natural resources: petroleum, natural gas, coal, chromium, copper, iron ore, lead manganese, zinc, sulfur.

Agriculture: wheat, rice, other grains, sugar beets, fruits, nuts, cotton, dairy products, wool, caviar.

Industry: petroleum, petrochemicals, textiles, cement and building materials, food processing (particularly sugar refining and vegetable oil production), metal fabricating (particularly steel and copper), armaments. It is the largest producer of steel and automobiles in the Middle East although domestic demand exceeds production.

Trade (2010 est): Because of lack of refining capacity, the country is highly dependent on gasoline imports (40% of domestic consumption or $5 billion in 2006).

Exports: $109.5 billion (2011 est): petroleum (80%), chemical and petrochemical products, fruits and nuts, carpets, pistachio nuts, saffron, fruits, caviar; Partners: China (21%), India (9.3%), Japan (8.9%), South Korea (7.9%).

Imports: $74.1 billion (2012 est): Industrial supplies, capital goods, foodstuffs and other consumer goods; Partners: UAE (31%), China (17%), South Korea (8%), Germany (5%), Turkey (4%).

Petroleum Sector: Iran is the second largest OPEC oil producer (third largest proven reserves); output averaged

76

about 4 million barrels per day in recent years. Revenues from oil exports accounted for about 60% of government revenues in 2011/12 and about 80% of foreign exchange.[14] The government owned National Iranian Oil Company (NIOC) is the largest and most important economic enterprise in the country, ranking as the third largest oil company in the world. A rise in world oil prices in 2011 increased Iran's oil export revenues by roughly $28 billion over 2010, easing some of the financial impact of international sanctions. Iran has been

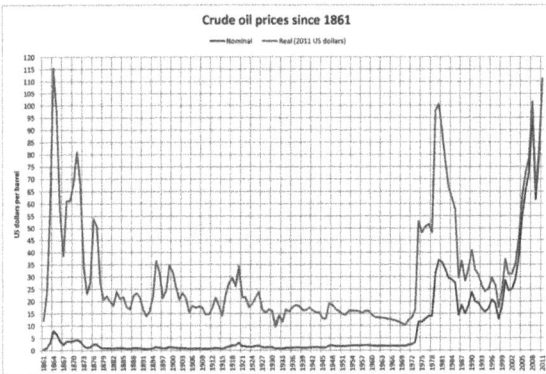

Figure 13 Crude oil prices.

[14]Iran has 15% of the world's natural gas reserves (as of 2008) but has been unable to become a major exporter of gas and has been a net importer as of 2005 through Turkmenistan.

77

working to reduce its dependence on oil export revenues by building up other sectors of its economy. (Adapted from World Bank, CIA Factbook and CRS RL 34525).

Government Economy Policy and Outlook (World Bank, October 2012): Iranian authorities have adopted a comprehensive strategy envisioning market-based re-

GDP Growth (Annual %)

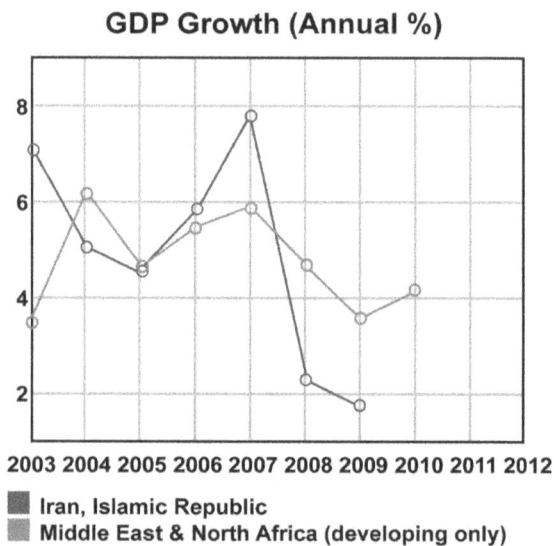

2003 2004 2005 2006 2007 2008 2009 2010 2011 2012

■ Iran, Islamic Republic
■ Middle East & North Africa (developing only)

Figure 14 Goss Domestic Product chart.

78

form as reflected in the Government's 20-year Vision document and Iran's fifth Five-Year Development Plan (FYDP, 2011–15). The Government envisioned a large privatization program in its 2010 to 2015 five-year plan aiming to privatize some 20% of state-owned enterprises (SOEs) each year. However, the Iranian Revolutionary Guards Corps, *Bonyads*, and other semi-Governmental enterprises have reportedly purchased controlling shares in numerous SOEs. The Government launched a major reform of its indirect subsidy system in December 2010. The Government opted for a direct cash transfer program while substantially increasing the prices of petroleum products, water, electricity, bread, and a number of other products.

The medium-term outlook for economic growth is negative due to the impact of stricter recent economic sanctions, which are expected to reduce revenues from oil exports and to impede corporate restructurings. The impact of recent sanctions is projected to push the economy into a recession in 2012. Stricter international economic sanctions, in particular the EU embargo on Iranian crude oil since July, led to a sharp decline in oil exports. The resulting (black market) depreciation of Iran's currency has contributed to increasing inflation. The official inflation rate has risen from 10% in 2010 to a 24% in 2012. For instance, Iran's sizeable pharmaceutical industry is reportedly struggling to import essential

79

raw materials. Moreover, the number of bankruptcies appears to be on the rise while factories are reported to be working at only half their capacity.

Bonyads **(Islamic Foundations/Trusts)** are semiprivate charitable Islamic foundations or trusts that are believed to wield enormous political and economic power in Iran. The largest *Bonyads* report directly to the Supreme Leader and are not subject to parliamentary supervision. Because *Bonyads* are not required to disclose their financial activities, it is not known exactly the magnitude of their wealth although they are believed to control up to 20% of Iran's economy.

The largest Iranian charitable trust is the Foundation of the Oppressed and War Veterans (*Bonyad e-Mostazafan va Janbazan,* MJF). With over 200,000 employees and 350 subsidiaries, the MJF has an estimated value of more than $3 billion, at least 10% of Iran's gross domestic budget (GDP). The MJF provides financial assistance, medical care, and recreational opportunities to Iran's poor and individuals wounded or disabled from the Iran-Iraq war. The MJF's domestic economic scope is expansive, with affiliates involved in economic areas such as agriculture, construction, industries, mining, transportation, commerce, and tourism. Since 1991, the MJF has invested in energy, business, engineering, and agricultural activities in Europe, Russia, Asia, the Middle East, and Africa. Some allege that the MJF is used for Iranian intelligence.

IRGC is involved in commercial activity in the construction, oil and gas, and telecommunications sectors and is believed to be the third largest economic enterprise in Iran, after the NOIC and MJF. The IRGC also controls defense-related enterprises and is said to serve as a leading investment vehicle for many of Iran's leaders. As noted, the IRGC is thought to be a major beneficiary of the recent privatization of government-owned enterprises and is thought to hold a controlling share in the newly privatized Telecommunication Company of Iran.

Social

Demographics: [15]
Population 78,868,711 (July 2012 est)
Population growth rate 1.247% (2012 est)
Median age is 27.4 years. (2012 est)
Life expectancy at birth: 70.35 years
Urbanization: 71% of population (2010)
Literacy: 77% over 15 years of age

[15] All statistics and estimates from https://www.cia.gov/library/publications/the-world-factbook/geos/sa.html

81

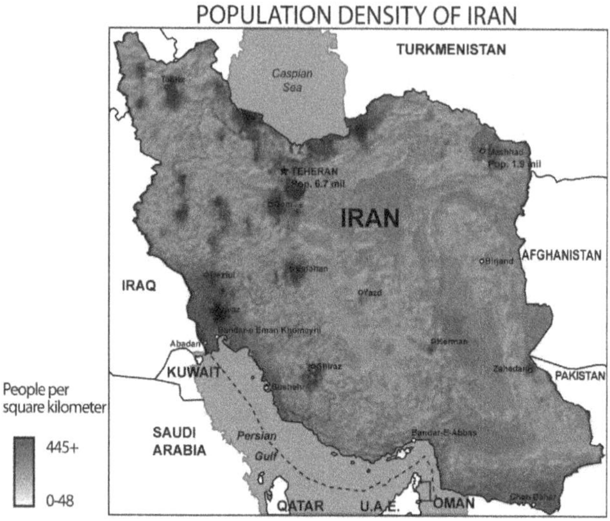

POPULATION DENSITY OF IRAN

Figure 15 Population density of Iran.

APRIL 2013

Population Bulge: About 34% of Iran's population is between the ages of 20 and 35 years of age.

Population Pyramid Graph - Custom Region - Iran

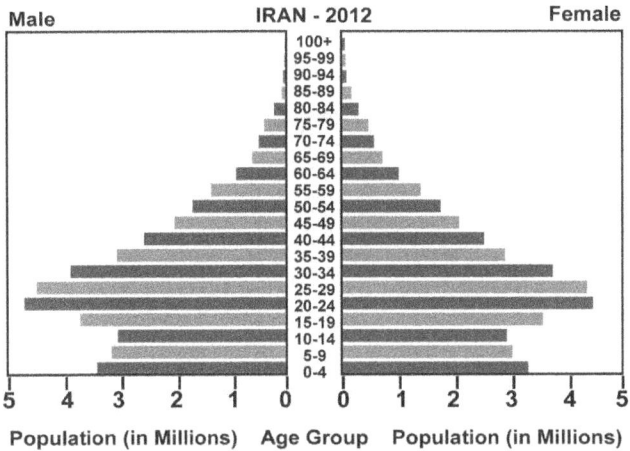

Figure 16 Population Bulge chart.

83

Language: The official language is Farsi (or Persian), which is an Iranian language spoken by 53% of the population in Iran. Farsi is written in Arabic script with the addition of four letters, which is referred to as Perso-Arabic. Variants of Farsi are Dari and Tajik.

Approximately18% speak Azeri Turkic or other Turkic dialects, 18% Kurd, 7% Gukaji and Mazandarani (Iranian Caspian languages), 6% Luri (Iranian language spoken in southwestern Iran), 2% Balochi, 2% Arabic, and 2% other.

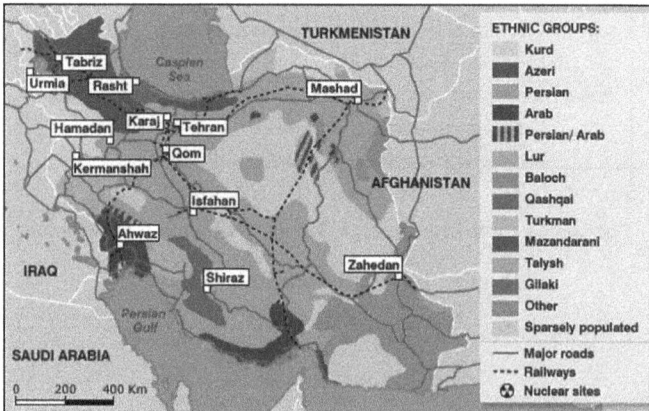

Figure 17 Ethnic groups in Iran.
https://blogs.law.harvard.edu/mesh/2009/04/persians-and-others-irans-minority-politics/

84

Education and Literacy: About 77% of the population is literate. Virtually all children of the relevant age group were enrolled in primary schools in 2009. Enrollment in secondary schools increased from 66% in 1995 to 84% in 2009. Youth literacy rates increased from 77% to 99% over the same period, rising significantly for girls (World Bank 2012)

Major Ethnic Groups: Persians account for a majority (61%) of the population of Iran. Minority ethnic groups include Azeri (16%), Kurd (10%), Luri (6%), Baloch (2%), Arab (3%), Turkmen and Turkic tribes (2%), and others (1%).

Azeris are the largest minority and are a Central Turkic peoples. Azeri Khanates historically were subject to Persian influence. After the Russian-Persian Wars (1812), the Azeris were divided between what is today Azerbaijan and Iranian Azeris, with the northern Azeri's eventually incorporated into the Russian Empire and the southern Azeris into what is today's modern Iran. Iranian Azeri elites have played important cultural and economic roles in Iran; the Iranian Azeri people have consistently been loyal to the Iranian state.

Kurds are the third largest minority group, mostly living in northwestern Iran adjacent to present day Kurdistan in

85

Iraq. Kurds have rebelled against Iranian rule since the 19th Century. Following the Iranian Revolution of 1979, a "holy war" called upon by the Ayatollah Khomeini crushed the Kurdish rebellion. In 2004, the Party for a Free Life in Kurdistan (PJAK) carried out a low level insurgency until December 2011, when a ceasefire was mediated by Iraqi Kurdistan Massoud Barzani. How-ever, clashes between the PJAK and IRGC have been reported through 2012.

Lurs are thought to be a mix of aboriginal and Iranian-Medes peoples. They have traditionally been tribal and pastoral nomads. The semi-autonomous position of the Lurs was crushed during the rule of the Pahlavi regime (1941-1979).

Balochis are a tribal nomadic people, having family and tribal ties with the larger Baloch populations in Pakistan and Afghanistan. They are mostly Sunni (Hanafi) Mus-lims with a strong cultural identity as Baloch. They oc-cupy sparsely populated mountains and deserts in south-east Iran. The Baloch groups, such as the *Jundallah* (Soldiers of God), are carrying on a low-level insur-gency against the Iranian government to establish a "Greater Baluchistan." Iranian officials allege *Jundal-lah* ties with *Al Qaeda*. The group is designated as a terrorist organization by Iran and the United States al-though several media reports allege the group receives support from the United States.

86

Arabs in Iran are mostly located along the Iraqi border in southeastern Iran in Khuzestan and south along the Persian Sea in Hormozgan province. In rural areas Arabs retain their tribal traditions. Iraq attempted to instigate a rebellion among the Iranian Arabs during the Iran Iraq war with no visible success.

Figure 18 Iranian Languages.

87

Class Structure: In spite of the Revolution's declared intention of doing away with Royalist class structure *(taghouti)*, Iran remains a class-conscious society. Iran is a hierarchical class society where subordination to family and political leadership is the norm. While the elite families, inner circles *(dovreh)*, and personal status are powerful forms of influence, the lower classes have produced more outstanding leaders since the revolution.

The greatest structural divide, outside of ethnicity and religion, is that of the rural-urban divide. Income and educational levels are at least twice as high in urban areas than in rural areas. This gap has lessened under the Islamic Republic. However, rural and urban income differences has again widened under Ahmadinejad, possibly (according to Brookings Institute, 29 Jan 2009) because of higher inflation working against those with below median incomes. Income inequality, as measured by the GINI index, is 44.5, slightly less than in the United States (45.0) but greater than Egypt (34.4).

88

Infrastructure[16]

Transportation:
Major Ports and Terminals: Assaluyeh, Bandar
Abbasm Bandar-e Eman Khomeyni

Figure 19 Ports of Iran.

[16]All statistics and estimates from https://www.cia.gov/library/
publications/the-world-factbook/geos/sa.html

89

Waterways: 850 km (on Karun River: some navigation on Lake Urmia) (2012)
Airports: 324 (2012). With paved runways: 136
Heliports: 21 (2012)

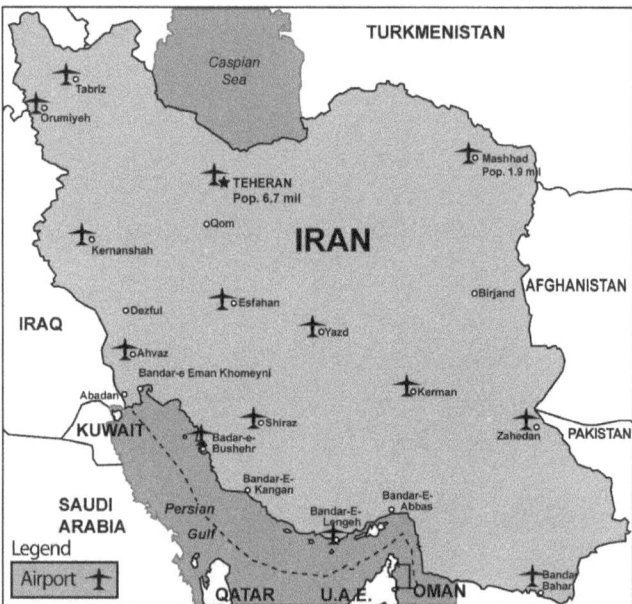

Figure 20 Airports of Iran.

90

Roadways: 172,927 km total
Paved: 125,908 km (includes expressway: 1429 km)
Unpaved: 41,019 km (2006)

Figure 21 Roadways of Iran.

91

Railways: 8442 km total
Broad gauge 94 km, 1676-m gauge
Standard gauge 8328 km (148 km electrified) (2008)

Figure 22 Railways of Iran.

Pipelines (2010):
Condensate/gas 12
Gas 20,155 km
Liquid petroleum gas 570 km
Oil 7123 km
Refined products 7927 km

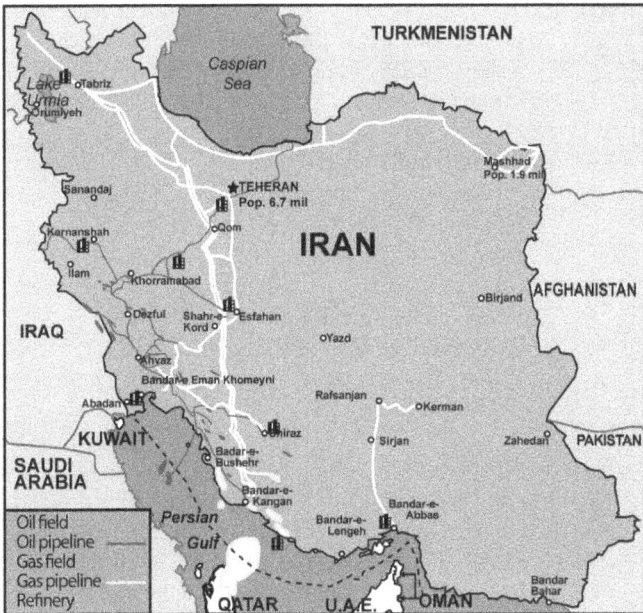

Figure 23 Oil and Gas pipelines of Iran.

93

Energy:
Electricity production: 213.7 billion kWh (2010 est),
export 6.2 billion kWh (2009 est)
>From fossil fuel: 81.4%
>Hydroelectric: 13.7%
>Other: 4,9%
Crude Oil
>Production: 4.231 million bbl/day (2011 est)
>Exports: 2.295 million bbl/day (2009 est)
>Proven Reserves: 151.2 billion bbl (1 January
2012 est)
Refined Petroleum Products
>Production: 1.801 billion bbl/day (2008 est)
>Exports: 246,500 bbl. day (2011 est)
>Imports: 187,200 bbl/day (2008 est)
Natural Gas
>Production: 146.1 billion cu m (2010 est)
>Consumption: 144.6 billion cu m (2010 est)
>Proven Reserves: 33.07 trillion cu m (1 January
>2012 est)

Health: Health indicators are above regional averages.
This success is attributed to effective delivery of primary health care, which almost balanced health care
outcomes in rural and urban areas (World Bank 2012).
The World Health Organization (WHO) ranks Iran's
overall health system performance in 2000 as 93rd out

APRIL 2013

of 191 countries, about the same as Indonesia and Panama.

The Ministry of Health and Medical Education (MOHME) is the main healthcare provider in Iran and runs a government network of hospitals and clinics (accounting for about 70% of hospital beds).

According to the Statistical Center in Iran the country has 730 hospitals and clinics with a total of 110,797 beds in 2003 or about 1.7 beds per 1000 population, and about 20,000 village clinics. WHO reports health care access as 86% in rural areas and 100% in urban areas. There is a reported 100,000 physicians (of which 46% are women) or about .75 per 1000 population. The government provides a "comprehensive insurance plan" to provide basic coverage.

About 96% of pharmaceuticals in terms of quantity (63% in terms of value) are produced locally. Lower-end medical equipment also is produced in Iran and exported to Iraq, Afghanistan, and Russia.

Water and Sewage: Iran has a modern infrastructure of dams, reservoirs, pipelines, and wells for delivering

fresh water. Traditional *karez* (Arabic: *qanat*) under-
ground canals are still in use in some rural areas.[17]
About half of the Iran's agricultural area is irrigated
while the other half is rain feed.

The World Bank in 2005 estimated that while about
98% of Iran's urban population is connected to public
water supplies, only 23% have access to public sewage,
of which only a "very small share" is treated. Some of
the sewage contaminates water supplies. The World
Bank provided support for water and sewerage projects
in Iran in early and the middle of the last decade.[18]

Each province has a water and wastewater company
responsible for water and sewage. Policy is set by the
Deputy Ministry of Water Affairs and eleven regional
water boards under the Ministry of Energy.

---

[17]The Associated Press recently reported that Iran launched a $1.5
billion project to move water through a 300 mile pipe from the
Caspian Sea to the Kavir desert for drinking and irrigation. [Associate
Press, Iran Launches $1.5B Water Project From Caspian Sea. April
26, 2012. http://news.yahoo.com/iran-launches-1-5b-water-project-
caspian-sea-104539767.html (accessed November 2012)]
[18]World Bank discontinued lending activities in Iran after 2005 in
compliance with sanctions.

INFORMATION

Telecommunication Infrastructure: The telecommunication sector is dominated by the Ministry of Communication and Information Technology.

Fiberoptic Network: Over 120,000 kilometers with connections to neighboring countries including UAE

Satellite. Iran is planning to launch a communication satellite in a venture with Russia. As of 2007, there are reportedly 13 earth stations (nine Intelsat and four Inmarsat).

Telephone:
Land line in use: 27.767 million (2011)
Mobile Cellular: 56.043 million (2011) (estimated to be over 80 million by 2013)

Internet:
Internet users: 8.214 million (2009)
Internet hosts: 167,453 (2010) Internet service is reported to be available in all major cities. Personal computer ownership is 10.5 per 100 people.

APRIL 2013

Broadcast Media:

Television broadcast stations: 29 plus 450 repeaters (1997)
Television sets: 15 million (2007 est)
Radio broadcast stations: 72 AM, 5 FM, 5 short-wave
Radio sets: 22 million (2007 est)

Islamic Republic of Iran Broadcasting (IRIB), the state-run TV broadcaster, operates 5 nationwide channels, a news channel, about 30 provincial channels, and several international channels. IRIB operates 8 nationwide radio networks, a number of provincial stations, and an external service.

About 20 foreign Persian-language television (TV) stations broadcasting on satellite TV are capable of being seen in Iran. Satellite dishes are illegal. While their use has been tolerated, authorities began confiscating satellite dishes following the unrest stemming from the 2009 presidential elections.

The Telecommunication Company of Iran (TCI) has a monopoly over telephone landlines and about 70% share of the mobile market. TCI has recently been privatized. Media reports TCI was sold to Mobin Trust Consortium, thought to be affiliated with the IRGC.

98

Internet and Social Media: In 2008, the Work Bank estimated that 32 percent of the population accessed the Internet and mobile phone use was greater than 65% of the population. The primary internet service provider (ISP) is the Telecommunication Company of Iran, with 50 private ISPs that must register with the government and employ a filtering system. Blogging, Twitter, Facebook, and text messaging are popular (RAND). In 2009, the Iranian Government actively sought to monitor, restrict, and censor access to the Internet content. Iran is developing a national internet (similar to North Korea, Myanmar, and Cuba), which is separate from the World Wide Web.

Print Media: The press is mostly privately-owned but subject to monitoring and control by the government Press/Media Supervisor Board under the Ministry of Culture and Islamic Guidance. A number of reformist newspapers have been closed since 2009. Newspapers of note are:

> *Iran* - official government newspaper with an English language edition, Iran Daily.
> *Kayhannder* – under the Office of the Supreme Leader.
> *Ettekaaat* - oldest newspaper in print now publ ished out of New York.
> *Etemaad* - reformist newspapers affiliated with

the political party, National Trust Party.
Ressalat - printed by the Islamic Educational
Foundation.
Tehran Times - an English language paper
owned by the Islamic Ideology Dissemination
Organization as the "voice of the Islamic Revo
lution."

The major news agencies are the government-owned
Islamic Republic News Agency (IRNA), the independent Fars News Agency, which the Wall Street Journal
reported is affiliated with the Revolutionary Guard, and
the *Mehr* News Agency, owned by the Islamic Ideology
Dissemination Organization. The Iran *Dokht* is an independent online platform with contributing writers.

Public Perceptions: We do not have reliable data on
Iranian public perceptions. There have been a series of
surveys conducted via phone to poll Iranians. The findings of these polls have been fairly consistent. However, these polls are unlikely to be based on true prob-
ability samples and phone lines are subject to monitoring. The polls do paint a picture somewhat at odds with
American media reports and are worth keeping in mind.
In general, the poll findings are:

- A majority of respondents view the economy as being "average" or better.
- A majority of respondents did not view sanctions as having a negative effect on the economy.
- A majority favored the development of nuclear capability while they were somewhat divided on the development of atomic weapons (with perception of a United States threat correlating with support for development of atomic weapons).
- A majority of respondents opposed the reestablishment of ties with the United States.

In general, it appears that Farsi speaking Iranians remain strongly opposed to American military action in their country, which holds across major demographic groups. We have no reliable data on perceptions by sociocultural groups about attitudes towards regime Islamic policy, leaders, and methods, which are critical to understanding internal sociocultural dynamics in Iran.

LOCAL UNITS OF MEASUREMENT
Length
   1 *arsani* or *ulna* = 52 to 64 cm.
   1 *chebel* = 40 *arsani* = 21 to 25 meters.
   1 *farsang (parasang)* = 6.23 km in 19th century
   Persia.
   1 *farsang* = 10 km in modern Iran and Turkey.
Volume
   1 *chenica* = 1.32 liters.

CALENDAR AND HOLIDAYS

Iran uses the Persian Solar year calendar (A.P.) for governmental and administrative purposes: a solar year is
350 days (which may vary from year to year by a day
from the Gregorian calendar). AP year 1391 began in
20 March 2012. Iran uses the Islamic Lunar calendar
(A.H.) for observing Islamic religious holidays: 2012 is
1433 A.H. The official public holidays are authorized
by the *Majlis* (Consultative Assembly) prior to the be-
ginning of the Iranian new year and dates below may not
be reliable.

Business hours are usually Saturday through Thursday,
0900 to 1700, with one hour usually for lunch. During

Table 3. Solar Holidays-National Secular

Solar Holidays – National Secular			
Persian	2013	English Name	Local Name
Farvardin 1	21 Mar	New Year Also known as "Nowruz"	عيد نوروز
Farvardin 2	22 Mar	Nowrooz	عيد نوروز
Farvardin 3	23 Mar	Nowrooz	عيد نوروز
Farvardin 4	24 Mar	Nowrooz	عيد نوروز
Farvardin 12	1 Apr	Islamic Republic Day	روز جمهوری اسلامی
Farvardin 13	2 Apr	Nature Day known as Sizde-Bedar (سیزده بدر)	روز طبیعت
Khordad 14	4 Jun	Khomeini's death	رحلت امام خمینی
Khordad 15	5 Jun	Revolt of Khordad 15	قیام ۱۵ خرداد
Bahman 22	10 Feb	Victory of the Iranian Revolution	پیروزی انقلاب
Esfand 29	20 Mar	Nationalization of Oil Industry	ملی شدن صنعت نفت

103

New Year's (Nowrooz), business and shops may close one week prior and one to two weeks following.

Nowrooz (Nowruz) is the secular traditional Persian New Year at the Spring Equinox usually occurring on 20 or 21 March, with festivities preceding and continuing to 1 April. Traditionally, a few weeks prior, Iranians conduct "spring cleaning" in their homes as part of the celebration of renewal. On the last Tuesday night of the old year, Iranians typically gather around bonfires to celebrate *Chahar Shanbeh Suri*, where jumping over the fire is to clean the body of *illness, bad feelings*, and *bad health*. The occasion is celebrated by families where it is traditional to give new crisp currency to children, gifts are exchanged, shopping for new clothes, relatives visited, and a holiday meal is prepared. Children may go to neighbors' homes for treats, like Halloween. The thirteenth day after the New Year, known as *Sizdah Bedar*, is traditionally spent outside the house heading for the parks or countryside for a picnic. Myth has it that the demon of drought is defeated at midday on *Sizdah Bedar*.

Shab-e yalda (Eve of *Yalda* ["birth"]) is the popular Persian celebration of the Winter Solstice, 21 and 22 December, but it is not an official holiday. It is an occasion for the extended family or friends to gather and share an evening meal. Traditionally, watermelon or other fruits or nuts are eaten, which are to ensure health and well-being. Typically, the participants stay up past mid-night and it will be an occasion for conversation, poetry reading and perhaps partaking of smoking the Gheylon (water pipe) and illicit alcoholic drinks. The occasion is traced back to the celebration of the birth of Mithra, a (perhaps, pre) Zoroaster divinity associated with the sun and symbolizes truth, light, and strength over the powers of darkness. After *shab-e yalda*, light-ness prevails. However, today the celebration has lost its original religious meaning.

Ramadan is the ninth month of the Islamic lunar calendar (based on lunar cycles) and the month that Muslims believe the *Qur'an* was first revealed to Muhammad. During *Ramadan*, Muslims fast (no food or water) from sunrise to sunset to purify themselves. Many mosques have a service that includes reading one-thirtieth of the *Qur'an* each night.

Fasting includes avoiding water, food, and sex, and re-fraining from all bad habits, words, places, and thoughts. Fasting during *Ramadan* is said to remind the faithful of the sufferings of the poor. In the evening after sunset, a meal is served to break the fast (the *Iftar* meal), and families and friends eat together.

105

Table 4 Lunar Holidays-Islamic

Islamic	2013	English Name	Local Name
Muharram 9	13 Nov	*Tasu'a* of Imam Hussain	تاسوعا
Muharram 10	14 Nov	*Ashura* of Imam Hussain	عاشورا
Safar 20	24 Dec	*Arba'een* of Imam Hussain	اربعين
Safar 28	11 Jan	Demise of prophet Muhammad and Martyrdom of Imam Hassan (Mujtaba)	وفات حضرت محمد و شهادت امام حسن مجتبی
Safar 29	12 Jan	Martyrdom of Imam Reza	شهادت امام رضا
Rabi'-ul-Awwal 17	29 Jan	Birth of Muhammad and Imam Jafar (Sadeq)	ولادت حضرت محمد و امام جعفر صادق
Jamaad-ath-Thaanee 3	13 Apr	Martyrdom of Fatima	شهادت حضرت فاطمه
Rajab 13	23 May	Birth of Imam Ali	ولادت حضرت علی
Rajab 27	6 Jun	Mission of Muhammad (Prophet's Ascension)	بعثت حضرت محمد
Sha'aban 15	24 Jun	Birth of Imam Mahdi	ولادت حضرت مهدی
Ramadhan 21	29 Jul	Martyrdom of Imam Ali	شهادت حضرت علی
Shawwal 1	8 Aug	Eid ul-Fitr (End of Ramadhan)	عید فطر
Shawwal 2	9 Aug	Eid ul-Fitr (Day After Ramadhan)	عید فطر
Shawwal 25	1 Sep	Martyrdom of Imam Jafar	شهادت امام جعفر صادق
Dh-ul-Hajja 10	15 Oct	Eid ul-Adha (Ghurban)	عید قربان
Dh-ul-Hajja 18	23 Oct	Eid al-Ghadeer	

106

Eid al-Fitr is the Festival of Breaking the Fast at the end of the month of *Ramadan*. It is somewhat like the festivities celebrated at the end of Easter/Lent to Christians. It lasts three days and is marked by eating meals, decorating the house, and exchanging gifts. Alms are given to the poor and people visit the mosque. The traditional greeting for *Eid* is *"Eid Mubarak,"* which means "blessed festival."

Eid al-Adha is the Feast of Sacrifice and occurs on the 10th day of the 12th month of the lunar calendar marking the end of the yearly *Hajj*. It is said to commemorate the sacrifice of a ram in place of Ismael (Ishmael) by Ibrahim (Abraham) as a supreme example of submission to *Allah.* Families that can afford it sacrifice a goat, camel, sheep, or cow and make a festive meal of it. They share the meat with the poor and needy.

Ashura is the Shia observance of *Ashura* and is one of the most important events in the Shia calendar. *Ashura* marks the anniversary of the martyrdom of Imam Husayn, son of Ali and grandson of the Prophet Muhammad. He and a small band of followers were killed and beheaded at Karbala in Iraq in 680 CE by the forces of the Caliph Yazid 1st.

107

PRIMER ON CROSS CULTURAL COMPETENCE

CULTURAL LITERATE SOLDIER

A cultural literate U.S. Army Soldier:
- Does not let personal prejudices cloud their judgment and determine their actions.
- Embraces our values while understanding how they may bias our decisions and action as perceived by those from other cultures.
- Acts with respect for the values, beliefs, and customs of other people.
- Knows the history, culture, and institutions of the people among whom the Soldier operates.
- Is able to take the perspective of those from other cultures.
- Has self-discipline to behave in a culturally appropriate way at all times.
- Can operate among people from other cultures with minimal cultural friction.
- Can appropriately greet, tactically direct, and know key native terms in the local language.
- Has the skills to effectively interact, avoid miscommunication, and build rapport to successfully achieve military tasks among peoples from other cultures.

APRIL 2013

- Positively influences people from other cultures to achieve mission objectives.
- Makes culturally informed decisions and has deep cultural situational awareness based on a sophisticated understanding of foreign cultures and structures.
- Incorporates cultural factors to effectively visualize, plan, and operate, which achieves mission success and minimizes unintended population consequences.

FUNDAMENTALS

Purpose: Each Soldier must be a culturally literate ambassador, aware and observant of local cultural beliefs, values, behaviors, and norms. Why?

- Understanding local culture allows for better decision making through a better and more holistic picture of the operational environment.
- It reduces friction between those with different cultural inheritance.
- It helps avoid underestimating potential adversaries.
- It allows better prediction and tracking of second and third order effects, helping to avoid unforeseen and unintended consequences.
- Leaders who acquire a basic understanding of local history and culture can also recognize and effectively counter propaganda, which misrepresents history.

APRIL 2013

- It allows for better operational planning and decision making.
- It can save lives.

Cross Cultural Competency is —
- *Cultural Knowledge:* Familiarization with cultural characteristics, population motivations (values, beliefs, attitudes, perceptions, and behaviors), and affiliation patterns of foreign nations, another ethnic group, or religious group needed for effective planning, targeting, and decision making.
- *Cultural Awareness:* Knowledge and appreciation of cultural differences/similarities, and cultural biases that minimize cultural friction.
- *Culturally Appropriate Skills:* The ways to effectively achieve tasks in a culturally appropriate way.
- *Foreign Language:* An ability to communicate in a foreign language to understand and direct non-English-speaking populations.

Understanding Culture: Culture is an interconnected set of ideas and feelings shared by a group—such as a clan, tribe, religious community, nation, or organization—that is passed from one generation to another. It is a belief tradition; for example, religious, intellectual, national, or folk. It establishes a common way of understanding the world (perspective) and what is important

110

(motivation). Without culture, every day would be a new challenge, forcing people to relearn and negotiate the rules for interacting with others. Culture establishes a common "software" (program) among a group towards which individuals in that group orient themselves, shaping their interactions. While each individual is unique, a shared set of ideas and ways of thinking drive a common group tendency in response to change.

Understanding culture is critical for population-centric military operations to (1) establish conditions and objectives, and (2) estimate population responses to our courses of action. Conditions needed to achieve policy goals can vary depending on the culture: conditions for establishing civil peace among tribes in Afghanistan can be substantially different from those between ethnic groups in Southern Thailand. Variations in perspectives and ways arising from a shared interconnected set of ideas can lead to differing responses to similar courses of action and differences in second and third order effects. Failure to include culture increases risk that military courses of actions will have unpredictable impact on the population.

Characteristics of culture:

- *Shared by a group* – there is no culture of one (which is psychology) .[19]
- *Learned* from interactions with a group.
- *Passed inter-generationally* that imparts continuity among a people over time.
- *Is an abstraction* (not a concrete "thing"), an inter-connected set of ideas to which people take as guides for their actions towards each other.
- *Based on symbols*, so meanings and perceptions are expressed through language, music, art, and other forms of symbolic expression.
- *Integrated* or holistic in that if one part changes, all the other parts react.
- *"Software"* shared by a group of people, programs that run the "hardware" of population structures and institutions.
- *Deeply embedded* and regarded as "normal" or "natural" by those within a group but as "odd" or even "offensive" by those outside the group.
- *Pervasive* – we often do not notice culture, because we take it for granted as "just the way things are."

[19]Culture is a commonly held set of beliefs "outside the head" to which individuals orient themselves and internalized "inside the head" (becoming part of one's psychology). Culture "outside the head" arises from symbols (like language or rituals) that are shaped by interactions and passed down across generations, evolving "outside the head" of any one individual.

112

Culture as "software" is distinct from institutions or "hardware." Understanding of both is needed to increase accuracy for estimating population effects. Institutions are how the population environment is organized, such as government, military organizations, businesses, or social groups (often expressed as PMESII). An analogy for how culture is related to institutions is how computer hardware is related to software – there are no outputs without both. In sociocultural analysis, both the group (hardware) and beliefs (software) are specified and analyzed to derive a dynamic (action).

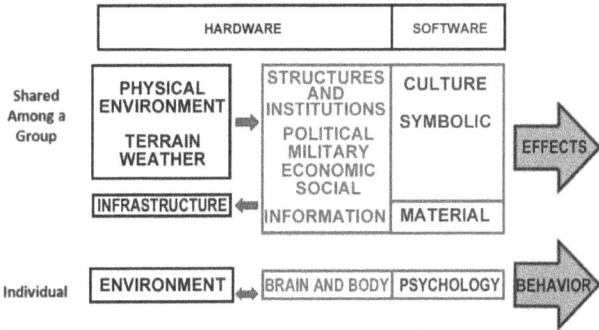

Figure 24 Hardware-Software flow chart.

113

Anthropologists typically conceptualize culture as *symbolic* culture and *material* culture. *Symbolic culture* is all of a group's ideas, symbols and languages. *Material culture* is tools, clothing, houses, and other things that people make or use. It is all human inventions: from stone tools to spacecraft.

CULTURAL AWARENESS

Cultural Bias

Since Americans share a world view based on our cultural inheritance, we are often blind to other perspectives. That is, from another cultural perspective, our views are culturally biased. Such cultural biases can obstruct gaining cooperation and support.

Cultural Prejudice is prejudging based on stereotypes (primarily crude second hand information)

Positive Prejudice – We admire aspects of other cultures whose values match with ours.

Negative Prejudice – We dislike aspects of other cultures that are opposed to our values.

Cultural Ethnocentrism is the assumption that one's own cultural values are natural and one's own cultural values are used to evaluate other cultures. To do so, implicitly leads to the belief in the superiority of one's own culture. Usually, one's own culture will be ranked higher than other cultures, and the converse is true (such as Americans judging Afghans by American values or Afghans judging Americans by Afghan values). Most everyone is ethnocentric to varying degrees. Lack of awareness of ethnocentricity can lead to cultural friction – misunderstanding and conflict.

115

American Cultural Values and Biases

- Our values can be seen from another cultural perspective as a bias: (American values – bias)
- **Democracy** – moral or religious authority not fully accessible to common wisdom.
- **Equality of opportunity** – importance of family and relationships.
- **Rule-oriented** – relationships and obligations.
- **American Dream (self-made man)** – importance of position in society.
- **Individual responsibility (self-attribution bias)** – situational bias.
- **Individual autonomy** – belonging to family or group.
- **Belief in progress** – tradition and past golden age.
- **Pragmatic (problems can be solved rationally)** – power of faith and ethical belief.

Cultural Stress Phases

We all initially experience cultural stress when first working in other cultures. Cultural stress arises when our cultural scripts (ways to act) and biases do not correspond to a foreign population, leading to cultural friction.

1. *Predeployment* (Honeymoon) – When first learning of deployment to another country, we generally have positive attitudes towards that culture.

116

2. *Initial contact* (Culture Shock) – When deployed and initially working with others from another culture, we find many of the cultural scripts do not work leading to a heightened sense of being American and negative views of those from other cultures.

3. *Adjustment* - After gaining greater experience,

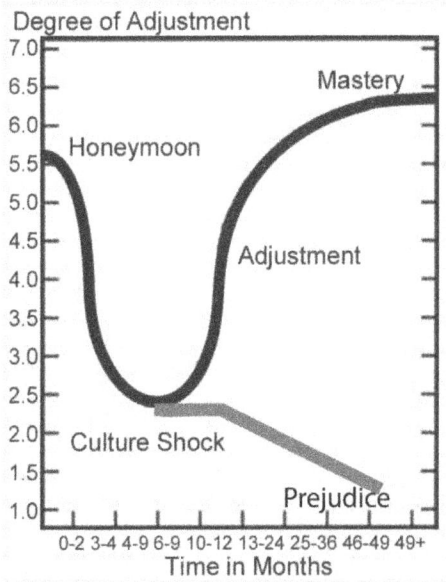

Figure 25 Degree of adjustment chart.

most of us learn to adjust our cultural scripts to become more effective when operating with others from a different culture. As effectiveness increases, our view of the other culture becomes more positive.

4. *Mastery or Prejudice* - Successful adaptation usually leads to positive views of the other culture and capability to act effectively. Unsuccessful adaptation leads to deepened dislike of the other culture and extremely negative views.

Indicators of Culture Shock:
- Anxiety – difficulty sleeping or relaxing.
- Vocal outbursts, dislike.
- Impatience, frustration, and distrust.
- Aggression.
- Growing ethnocentricity.
- Avoidance or discomfort with local nationals.

Managing Cultural Stress
Predeployment
- Identify as a cultural agile Soldier.
- Mission focus – population centric and importance of self-discipline.
- Cultural Awareness Training – familiarity with other cultures, demand respect, cultural stress cycle.

Deployment
- Actively monitor.
- Pair newbie with mentors.
- Command climate – demand respect and nontolerance for derogation.
- Cultural awareness training – learn local culture and ways to adapt.
- Refer extreme cases to professional care – behavior specialist or Chaplin.

Cultural Differences

Cultural Dimensions in most any culture can be understood in terms of —
- Values, beliefs, and identity - which include their history, morale, and religion.
- Behaviors - their customs/etiquette, ceremonies and rituals, use of body language, and personal space.
- Power distance - or acceptance of authority between superiors and subordinate.
- Forms of solidarity – what binds us together such as individualism and collectivism.
- Ways of thinking - time orientation, ways of reasoning, and decision making.
- Affect – appropriate display of feelings and meaning.
- Gender relations – roles, importance, and ways to interact.

Cultural Ideal-Types are abstractions, like feudalism, that help us understand the chaos that is reality and enables us to make decisions. Ideal-types enable us to navigate and fix what is important in a reality that is various. Three major cultural ideal-types are:

Ascriptive
- Social role is primary and ascribed by the family one belongs to.
- Roles are diffuse.
- Collectivist.
- Personal relationship-oriented.
- Consensual where age is valued.
- High Context – understanding the situation.
- Respect and honor are highly valued – sensitive to shame.
- Custom and tradition are highly valued.

Achievement
- Social role is achieved through merit or talent.
- Roles are specialized.
- Individualistic where autonomy is valued.
- Impersonal rational and contract-oriented.
- Competition and rule-oriented.
- Low Context– articulation and generalized logic are central
- Achievement is highly valued.
- Innovation and future orientation are highly valued.

120

Clientalistic
- Relationship is an instrumental friendship between a patron and client.
- Patron provides "gifts of authority" such as insurance, access, and advice.
- Clients provide "gifts of obedience" such as loyalty, granting prestige, and support.
- One establishes a network – chain of patron and clients.
- Relationship is established on the basis of private personal relationships, not contractual.
- There tends to be a transitional phase between ascriptive and achievement or when these types of cultures break down.

Incorporating Culture

Target to achieve desired effect

| Structural Variables | ➡ | Culture Factors | ➡ | Environmental-Cultural Effects |

Given PMESII   Population Perspective   Impact on Mission

Figure 26 Incorporating culture.

121

CULTURAL KNOWLEDGE

Recent military operations among foreign populations
have led to the rediscover of the importance of culture.
Lack of cultural awareness and knowledge has been
identified by the U.S. Army as a "critical gap" in capability.

Incorporating Culture into Military Operations: Historically, the U.S. Army focused on operating variables
that could be observed. Culture was largely absent because culture often could not be directly observed. The
resulting analysis often failed to account adequately for
population motivations and to accurately predict effects
of our courses of action or, in some cases, adequately
specify objectives concerning the population.

Culture is important to incorporate into military planning and decision making where population motivations
matter. Culture is the software or program that is shared
by a population and directs group level behavior. Population motivation is not only important for analyzing
society but also politics (political culture), military
(military culture), and the economy (cultural economics).

Political: To paraphrase, given that war is politics by
another means, understanding political culture is

122

crucial: the structure of power, authority and legitimacy on how decisions are made and conflicts adjudicated; and the populations' loyalty, identity, and obligation to groups or the state.

Military: Perhaps the most important consideration for military operations is military or security culture: the inherited ways to fight, historic threat perceptions, acceptable use of violence and war among the population, and how victory is defined.

Economic: Cultural economics is crucial to properly employ "money as ammunition": the population response; exploitation of traditional economic means and ways by the insurgency; and impact on traditional networks like patron-client, tribes, villages, and occupational groups.

Social: Sociocultural factors may also be important: impact on traditional and religious beliefs of a population, impact on gender relations, and sociocultural based grievances.

Cultural factors are considered in developing running estimates and initial assessments as well as in the analysis of mission variables and course of action development and assessment. In population-centric warfare or stability operations, population and cultural considerations are of primary importance. Cultural factors become more important to the extent that the local culture differs from that of the United States.

In conventional warfare, culture is less of a factor at the tactical level. It is still important to derive rules of engagement (ROE), no-strike lists, population movements caused by military operations, and a smooth transition to CMO. Cultural factors are an important factor to the extent that conventional war operations shape follow-on stability operations. Here, impact on population and political perceptions, enabling friendly local forces, and damage to infrastructure, and persistence of effects are likely to be important considerations.

Cultural factors are critical in COIN. Culture greatly shapes factors leading to population support; being exploited by the adversary to gain support, regeneration, discredit the government; establishing its infrastructure; and establishing the host government legitimacy. Cultural factors are equally important in stability operations where (1) political competition can be intense and all COAs may have political implications, and (2) civil security and stability can be established through strengthening local cultural sources of resilience.

124

APRIL 2013

Operating Environment - PMESII
Running Estimates

METT-TC

Human Dimensions	Population				System
	Area Structures	Events	People (Hardware)	Culture (Software)	Capabilities and Dynamics
Political Decision Making/Power		History Current Issues	Government Political Leaders Laws	Power Legitimacy Civic Culture	Competition Legitimacy Crisis Resistance
Military/Security Physical Force/Threat		History Current Issues	Order of Battle Doctrine Train Equipment	Warrior Culture Accept Violence Threat Perceptions	Morale Perception of Victory Security Attitudes
Economic Resources/Distribution		History Current Issues	Stucture Enterprises Income	Expectations Beliefs Traditional Practice	Grievances Conflict Resource Flow
Social Solidarity/Cleavages		History Current Issues	Demographics Group-Orgs. Communication	Identity Groups Social Status Affiliation Patterns	Grievances Resilience Polarization

Figure 27 METT-TC.

Cultural Data: Cultural data, broadly, are shared beliefs of and common patterns of affiliation among target population groups. Such data are typically derived from –

- Population engagements and interviews.
- Key cultural informants.
- MISO, CA, and HTT reports.
- Media and intelligence reports.
- Observational and patrol reports.
- Population surveys.

125

APRIL 2013

Histories, academic research, and NGO and government reports along with databases can also be sources of important data as well as analysis.

Care must be taken to not confuse analytical objectives with information categories. Frameworks, such as the PMESII, are functional or analytical. In stratified (and to some extent achievement) cultures, roles and functions are distributed so an individual may not fit in any one analytical category. Rather, these categories focus on analysis (such as power, force, resources, and solidarity/ cleavage) rather than usefulness for the categorization of data.

Cultural Analysis: Typical steps are —
- *Segment* population by shared sociocultural characteristics – drill down beyond demographics.
- *Match* belief and affiliational patterns to segmented sociocultural groups.
- *Identify* key groups for mission objectives.
- *Understand relation* of structure and beliefs/ affiliational patterns with group motivations relative to mission objectives.
- *Conduct a site assessment* to validate and collect data to refine analysis.
- *Refine analysis*: power structure, decision making, population power analysis, interactions.
- *Generate IR* – collect data and further refine analysis.

126

- *Estimate population impact of proposed* COAs, including second and possibly third order effects.
- *Monitor* population responses to operations – note difference from expected.
- *Conduct an after-action assessment*, collect data, and develop lessons learned.

CULTURAL-GENERAL CONCEPTS

Social Norms and *Mores* (mor-rays)

A *norm* is a range of behavior that is considered permissible by a particular group. Norms tell us how to behave in certain situations. They are social guidelines that most people follow. Norms are not rigid and may be ignored with only minor repercussions. For instance, being late to a meeting does not mean that you will be put in jail or killed. Norms are "social lubricants" that help people interact smoothly. Shaking hands, bowing, and greetings are all norms that help us relate to others. There are norms for behavior, gender relations, voice loudness and body language, and almost everyone conforms.

Mores are a wider category than norms and include both local etiquette and the fixed customs and fundamental moral views of a human group. Mores give guidance on how to think and behave.

Norms and mores tell us about core emotional beliefs such as child rearing practices, vengeance, the roles of patronage and corruption, or the roles of women and religion in daily life.

Culture acts as a form of glue to hold a group together; it does not stay the same—it changes over time as circumstances change. Culture defines us, but we also define culture. New events, technology, influences, and circumstances can all change our culture. Certainly, the invention of computers, the Internet, and instant communication has changed the culture of the average American. Culture reacts to technological change and is always influencing how we perceive change. It tells us who we are, but we reserve the right to modify our values, beliefs, behaviors, and norms (VBBNs) at any time to suit the circumstances.

Enculturation

Learning one's own culture is called *enculturation.* We learn the "proper way to do" things from a young age by growing up in a particular culture. We are taught the right way to behave and accomplish basic activities from parents, relatives, teachers, and friends. Today the Internet, movies, and television provide new channels for enculturation.

128

We learn most of the cultural rules unconsciously and assume that they are natural instead of culturally constructed. What we are taught at an early age becomes part of our thoughts and feelings, and often results in an unquestioning acceptance of cultural assumptions. All humans are acculturated into their group's culture, and they learn the "correct" ways of doing things and understanding the world around them.

Children in any culture are taught the "way things are": that is, "What" to eat, "How" to eat, what is "Good," who the "Gods and Goddesses" are, "Proper" etiquette and behavior, and so on. Children absorb the information that their parents, relatives, peers, and the media give them. We perceive our culture as simply "the way things are," making us like fish swimming in water. We swim in a sea of culture and generally do not even realize that it is supporting all we do.

Culture gives us both the values that we assume and the beliefs we use to talk about them. Together they form the norms of our society, and those norms influence the behavior of us all. Culture tells us what we are supposed to do or not do in any given situation.

Cultural Relativism

To avoid ethnocentrism and underestimation of potential adversaries, we must realize that a local society is based on its own culture and history.

Cultural relativism is the idea that different cultures as distinct and unique wholes have different values, beliefs, behaviors, and norms from one another, and hence see and respond to the world in different ways.

Cultural relativism does not mean moral relativism. Moral relativism asserts that there are no absolute standards for right or wrong. Therefore, one cannot judge anyone else or another culture as these standards vary according to culture, time, and situation. This means that we reserve judgment of other cultures' beliefs and behaviors until we have a thorough understanding of why they act and believe as they do, based on a clear understanding of their history, religion, technology, and environmental situations.

Cultural relativism helps to get beyond stereotypes and is a method to limit the negative impact of ethnocentrism.

Culture Shock

Culture shock is a feeling of dislocation, of being "out of place" in a new culture.

130

When arriving in an alien environment with new smells, new languages, new faces, and different types of clothing, along with new rules, Soldiers may commonly experience some culture shock. This can be particularly important if embedded with host nation forces.

After a long deployment or several deployments, a Soldier can experience *reentry* shock (reverse culture shock) upon returning home. He/she finds that it does not meet expectations or memories, since things have changed in his/her absence. If not recognized as part of a normal return experience, this can lead to depression. It is important to recognize culture shock and reentry shock, to discuss them with friends, and, if the conditions continue, to seek help and counseling.

Culture shock sometimes leads Soldiers to reexamine their values, priorities, and what they think of themselves and the U.S. This also happens when returning home after a long absence. Reentry to home culture after a long absence can be difficult since people cannot simply pick up their lives where they left off. People and the culture at home have changed during your absence.

There are many techniques for coping with culture shock and reentry shock. The best way to minimize culture shock is to educate yourself about the culture to which you are being deployed by reading books, seeing

131

films, and talking with natives and people who have been there. Talking about your feelings with others also helps. Reentry shock, or returning to your familiar society, also requires adjusting to the changes in oneself and those that have occurred in the home culture while absent.

Social Taboo

Taboos are *mores* specifying what actions are prohibited in a culture. Taboos are activities or uses of physical objects that are explicitly forbidden and are based on religious notions of what is and what is not permissible.

Drinking coffee for Mormons and eating pork for Jews and Muslims are all examples of food taboos. These taboos create boundaries between people and constantly remind believers that they belong to a certain group with group expectations.

Most cultures have an incest taboo prohibiting having sexual relations with close relatives, but different cultures may define who close relatives are differently. In most American states you cannot marry your uncle, aunt, niece, or nephew. In past American Indian cultures a preferred marriage was one between one's mother's brother's children. In some traditionally Islamic Middle East cultures, the preferred marriage pattern has been to

132

marry one's father's brother's daughter. This keeps within the larger family the bride price that is paid to the father of the daughter. (See —Local Kinship Systeml, below).

Rites of Passage

All cultures celebrate the events of birth, coming of age, marriage, and death. These and other rites of passage mark changes in a person's status. Rites of passage include boot camp/basic training, *quinceanera* (a Hispanic girl turns 15), *Bar/Bat Mitzvahs*, graduation ceremonies, and funerals. Rites of passage usually include three stages:

> **First Stage:** The separation of the inductees from the normal population as in basic training where inductees get haircuts and new clothes.
> **Second Stage:** The in-between stage where the inductees go through a period of training and tests as in the four years it usually takes to get a college degree.
> **Third Stage:** The inductees reenter the normal population but now with a new status as a graduate, a married person, or an adult.

Rites of passage can teach you much about a culture. In the Islamic world the most important rites of passage are marriage and the *Hajj* to Mecca. After completing the pilgrimage to Mecca, a person's new status is that of *Hajji.*

133

Tribe
Tribe is a term that is often misused. Generally, tribe refers to a range of kinship-based groups that are politically integrated under some unifying factor, such as leaders, geography, language, or history, and share or assume to share a common ancestry. Tribes stress that all men are equal but in some tribes, "Big Men" have more influence than others. Leaders or tribal councils have little ability to enforce decisions. Often tribe is just one factor in a person's identity. Tribal conflicts often occur over resources such as when two different tribes claim grazing land, trees on a mountain, or minerals.

Local Kinship System
Families are formed through marriage, and marriage serves economic and social functions. Two or more families united through marriage can form alliances. Kinship refers to the relationships that are based on relatedness through descent and marriage. For tribes and much of the non-industrial world, kinship is the single most important fact of life. Identity, rights, obligations, status, and survival depend on kin. Kin often share resources, defend each other against outsiders, and intermarry.

Marriage is the bedrock of kinship and is a legal, sexual, and economic union between men and women such that the children born to the woman are recognized as legitimate offspring of the parents. Marriage in the West revolves

134

around romantic love, but traditionally, marriage was an economic alliance between families or groups. People do not just get married to their spouse; they also assume obligations to their in-laws. In many parts of the Middle East couples tend to reside at the house of the husband's father, and a wife is under the close supervision of her mother-in-law until the wife produces a son.

Many families around the world are headed by a senior man and his wife, their married sons and daughters, and unmarried sons and daughters. Anthropologists refer to this as an extended family. This keeps the costs of marriage down and the bridewealth/brideprice in the family. Bridewealth is the opposite of dowry, which is payment to the groom's family.

In pastoral and farming societies, kin are often organized into extended families, lineages, clans, and tribes. Lineages are generally groups of people who interact regularly and know the genealogical connections. Clans are groups of lineages that are so large they may only interact once a year and do not know all the genealogical connections. Clans solve this problem by saying "We are all descendants of X." "X" may be a person or a totem animal. A totem animal is a way of bringing solidarity to a group with few political connections. The people believe they are all descendants of a human or animal

135

spirit or ancestor. These spirits can be helpful or jealous and wrathful. Clans usually hold religious rites once or twice a year, which allows for people to meet and be married from different clans. War is another reason clans may come together—to defend communal territory.

Nepotism is common in much of the world, and it is seen as natural that people take care of their children and friends. Networks of family members and friends can be analyzed and plotted, and this can be a powerful COIN technique.

136

References and Suggested Reading:

Abrhamian, Evand. *A History of Modern Iran.* Cambridge University Press, 2008.

Arjomand, Said Amir. *After Khomeini: Iran Under His Successors.* Oxford University Press, 2009.

Bar, Shmuel, Iran: *Cultural Values, Self Images and Negotiation Behavior,* IPS Institute for Policy and Strategy, 2004

Cordesman, Anthony H. *"Iran and the Threat to "close" the Gulf.* Center for Strategic and International Studies, 30 Dec 2011.

Eisenstadt, Michael. *The Strategic Culture of the Islamic Republic of Iran: Operational and Policy Implications.* Marine Corps University, 2011. http:// www.washingtoninstitute.org/ uploads/Documents/ opeds/4e60ff471079a.pdf.

Hooman Majd, *The Ayatollah begs to Differ: The Paradox of Modern Iran.* Anchor, 2008.

Keddie, Nikki R. and Yann Richard, *Modern Iran: Roots and Results of Revolution.* Yale University Press, 2003.

Koutlaki, Sofia, *Among the Iranians: A Guide to Iran's Culture and Customs,* Intercultural Press, 2010.

Mackey, Sandra Mackey. *The Iranians: Persia, Islam and the Soul of a Nation,* Plume, 1998

APRIL 2013

Mottahedeh, Roy, *The Mantle of the Prophet, 2nd Edition.* Oneworld, 2008.

Nateghpour, Mohamad Javad, *Islamic Councils and Social Democracy in Iran,* Welt Trends, 44:12, 2004, pp.61-73.

Nichioruk, Brain, Jerrold D. Green, Frederic Wehrey, Alireza Nader, and Lydia Hansell, *The Rise of the Pasdaran: Assessing the Domestic Roles of Iran's Islamic Revolutionary Guards Corps.* RAND, 2009.

Polk, William R. *Understanding Iran: Everything You Need to Know, From Persia to the Islamic Republic, Know, From Persia to the Islamic Republic, From Crus to Ahmadinejad.* Palgrave Macmillian, 2011.

Price, Massoume, *Iran's Diverse Peoples: A Reference Sourcebook.* 2005.

Takeyh, Ray, *Guardians of the Revolution: Iran and the World in the Age of the Ayatollahs.* Oxford University Press, 2009.

Ward, Steven R. *Immortal: A Military History of Iran and its Armed Forces.* Georgetown University Press, 2009.

Wright, Robin. *The Iran Primer: Power, Politics, and U.S. Policy.* United States Institute of Peace & Woodrow Wilson Center, 2010.

U.S. Government, Central Intelligence Agency. *World Factbook: Iran.* https://www.cia.gov/library/publications/the-world-factbook/geos/ir.html

APRIL 2013

Notes

APRIL 2013

Notes

Notes

Notes

Notes